Who Harnessed the Horse?

The Story of Animal Domestication

by Margery Facklam

Illustrated by Steven Parton

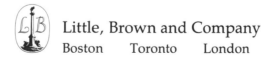

Little, Brown and Company
Boston   Toronto   London

For Daniel Francis Thomas,
with love
from his grandma

First Edition

Library of Congress Cataloging-in-Publication Data

Facklam, Margery.
  Who harnessed the horse? : the story of animal domestication /
by Margery Facklam ; illustrated by Steven Parton. — 1st ed.
    p.   cm.
  Includes index.
  Summary: Illustrates the ways in which humans and animals have
worked together throughout history, from the dogs that helped Stone
Age people hunt to bacteria that gobble up oil spills.
  ISBN 0-316-27381-3
  1. Domestic animals — History — Juvenile literature.
  2. Domestication — History — Juvenile literature. [1. Domestic
animals — History.   2. Domestication — History.]   I. Parton, Steven,
ill. II. Title.
  SF41.F33 1992
  636'.009 — dc20   91-13079

10 9 8 7 6 5 4 3 2 1
HAL

Published simultaneously in Canada
by Little, Brown & Company (Canada) Limited

Printed in the United States of America

Contents

Who Harnessed the Horse?

1
Man's First Best Friend

A wolf howled. Another answered, and another, until a chorus of howls echoed through the night. A young boy shivered. He inched closer to his little sister, who had grabbed most of their skimpy fur cover. The fire in the cave entrance crackled as a log shifted. Flames cast long shadows that danced like ghosts on the jagged rock walls. The wolves always lurked closer to the cave after the boy's clan had feasted on a big kill. In the firelight, the boy saw one wolf dart in to snatch a bone. Its eyes glowed like the full moon. A second wolf snapped at the bone. They growled, and each wolf tugged until a chunk of meat ripped off. Then, both satisfied, they trotted away.

The boy's father grunted. He pulled his elk-skin cloak around him and went back to snoring. The boy was just dozing off when he heard a noise — a whimper. Was it a dream? The noise was closer the second time, and he felt something nuzzle his foot. Some small cave animal, the boy decided. He pulled his bare foot under the fur cover.

When the first rays of sun warmed the cave the next morning, the boy found a wolf cub curled next to him. The boy moved, and the cub woke up. It glanced around fearfully, as though wondering what it was doing so close to the strange scent of humans. The boy reached out to touch it, and the cub darted away.

All day the boy and his sister searched, but it was not until dark that they saw the young wolf again. It cast a small shadow in the firelight, but its eyes glowed like the big wolves'. Why was it alone? Was it lost? The boy tossed it a scrap of meat, and the wolf swallowed it in one gulp. After that, the boy and his sister saw the cub often. When three full moons had come and gone, the clan headed for a new hunting ground in a warmer place, and the young wolf followed.

In another part of the world, three children were splashing in a puddle at the edge of the forest when they heard the shouts of men coming back to camp. The hunters were bringing food! The women and children ran to meet them. Four men dragged a buck antelope they had snared in a trap. Two other men struggled with a bulky sack made from an animal skin. It seemed alive with shifting lumps and bumps. When the men dumped the sack on the ground, six pudgy wolf cubs tumbled out, all yipping and yelping. The women had already poked a circle of sticks firmly into the dirt to make a pen where the cubs would be kept and fattened for tender meals in the days ahead.

During the next few weeks, it was the children's job to feed

the young wolves. The fattest pups were eaten first, of course, until only the *runt* of the litter was left. A small girl had been feeding the tiny wolf extra bits of meat she'd saved from her own portion. One evening she asked her father if she could keep the wolf. Did he say yes? Did he decide that she could have this wolf for a friend?

Nobody really knows who made the first wolf friend, but it probably happened over and over again in different places. Wolf cubs are easy to tame, and once tamed, they are loyal to the person who takes the place of their pack leader. It was these tamed wolves that became the *ancestors* of all dogs. And they changed forever the way humans live.

The dog's family story began more than twenty thousand years ago in a time called the *Stone Age*. People hadn't yet learned how to plant seeds and raise crops. They walked from place to place to find food. They had no animal companions — no horses to ride or cows to milk. Wherever these wandering people found a cave or shelter near a water hole, they made camp. They hunted animals they could kill with spears or clubs or snare in traps, and they gathered plants for food and medicine. As the seasons changed, they followed herds of animals that also moved to better feeding grounds.

Wolf packs are a lot like human families. A pack lives in a territory with one leader, usually an older male wolf. Like those early human hunters, wolves also follow herds of grazing animals. They work together to surround and kill one animal from a herd, and they share food with all their pack members.

4

When wolves can't find one animal big enough to feed them all, they eat small animals or scavenge the kills of other animals. It was a lucky day for humans when hungry wolves discovered that people threw away their leftovers. Wolves that stayed close to camps and caves to paw through garbage could be tamed. And slowly, over thousands of years, these tamed wolves began to change into the first domestic animals — dogs.

All dogs come from wolves. How did that happen? How could a three-pound Chihuahua, a wiener-shaped dachshund, a fluffy poodle, and a sleek greyhound have come from the same wolf ancestor?

No one knows exactly when some of the tamed wolves had changed so much that they became known as dogs, but we do know why. Some of the changes came about because tamed wolves didn't have to fend for themselves. An animal that is

fed and protected can survive without the same skills and equipment that a wild animal needs. It doesn't have to work as hard to catch food, and it doesn't have to be as wary of enemies or as keen to protect a territory. A German shepherd has about 220 million smelling cells in its nose. That's a million times better than ours, but it's not as good as a wolf's. A dog also has fewer and smaller teeth than a wolf, and this is one way scientists can tell the difference between the two *species* when looking at fossils.

Other changes came about when wolves of one kind met wolves of another kind as they traveled with wandering humans. Like us, wolves come in a variety of sizes, colors, and temperaments. In one litter there may be a black wolf, a gray one, a reddish brown one, and a blond. One may be timid, and another bold and fearless. One may grow up to be a leader, another a hunting scout, and another a good baby-sitter for the cubs. As the tribes of hunters and gatherers from the Middle East trekked across wide plains and high mountains, they met other wandering people. The small, slender wolf-dogs that traveled with them met and mated with the larger, thick-coated wolves from northern lands. The cubs they had would have been a combination of both kinds of wolves, resulting in different sizes, temperaments, thicknesses of fur, or combinations of colors.

The earliest known dog bones, different in size and shape from a wolf's bones, were found in the Middle East and date back more than ten thousand years. Fossil bones of two later kinds of domestic dogs were found farther north in Denmark. The size and shape of those 9,500-year-old bones seemed to suggest that these dogs had come from a mixture of large northern wolves and smaller wolf-dogs of the south.

Already different from their wolf ancestors in many ways, dogs changed most as people found different uses for them. When a man saw a long-legged dog that ran like the wind or a dog that could follow the scent of a rabbit better than any other, he wanted more dogs like that to help him hunt. People who needed big, tough dogs to guard their camps probably looked for the biggest, roughest male and female dogs to produce puppies of the same kind. In other words, people began to deliberately choose dogs because they had certain *traits*. A trait is some quality or appearance such as height, color, shape, or temperament. No one can give an animal a trait that wasn't already there in the first place. A trait can only be made stronger by *selective breeding*. A dog is selected for some reason — speed, good sense of smell, or keen hearing, for example. Then it is mated to a similar dog to pass that trait along. Traits are not added to an animal by selective breeding, but some traits may be exaggerated. Selective breeding is what makes the difference between a tame animal and a *domesticated* animal.

Tame animals are simply animals that are no longer wild. They may depend on people for food and shelter, but otherwise they haven't changed at all. Domesticated animals are also tame, but they have been changed deliberately to suit humans' purposes.

At first, tamed wolves of the north may have been penned up until people needed them to help catch and kill a reindeer. Of course the fastest wolves were selected for such work. When people discovered that their wolf-dogs were eager to please and willing to work together as a team, they harnessed the animals to pull sleds across ice and snow. Today's sled-dog breeds, such as Eskimo huskies and Alaskan malamutes, are still the most wolflike. Sometimes sled-dog owners will let their dogs loose to mate with wild wolves. But it's easy to tell the difference between a sled dog and a wolf by looking at their tails. A wolf's tail is never curled up over its back like a sled dog's.

Wolves and sled dogs are an easy comparison. But how did

dogs get to look like a wiener or have a pushed-in bulldog face or droopy ears? How did they get curly hair or no hair at all? The answer is *mutation* (mew-TAY-shun). A mutation is a chance of nature that causes an animal to be born slightly different from others of its kind. One pup might be born with a short, pushed-in snout, for example. Some of that dog's pups could also have that same short snout, and the new trait would be passed along, or *inherited*. But no matter what kind of bulldog face or wrinkly skin or other mutation may occur, all dogs are built on the basic plans of the wolf.

In ancient Egypt, seven thousand years ago, people raised the saluki, a dog that could outrun the fastest gazelle. It's said to be "as old as time itself." Some claim it is the first known *breed*. A breed is a variety of animal within a species. Like its close cousin the greyhound, the saluki still hunts with its sharp eyes instead of its nose. Egyptians called the saluki "the noble one." In ancient times these dogs were never sold, but they were exchanged for camels and other valuables from Arab traders. The saluki was the only dog ever allowed to sleep in the tent of an Arab sheik. Mummies of these pet dogs have been found buried in tombs of ancient Egyptian kings. On the collar of one dog was its name, Grabber, and another was called Cooking Pot. It's easy to guess what kind of dog Grabber might have been. But did Cooking Pot hang around the kitchen so much that the cook threatened to throw him in the pot, perhaps?

The Afghan hound is also a very old breed. It has been called the "dog of Noah's ark." Six thousand years ago, these tall, slender hounds herded flocks of sheep. They were courageous guards that could fight a leopard if they had to. One Egyptian king had two thousand slaves just to take care of one favorite Afghan hound.

White- and black-spotted Dalmatians trotted after chariots four thousand years ago in Egypt. Centuries later they followed gypsy caravans in Europe, where they got their name, from the region called Dalmatia in Austria. Through the years they've been used as retrievers and trackers, as sentries and shepherds, and even as clowns in circuses. But they are best known today as "firehouse dogs." Dalmatians have been comfortable with horses since they ran after chariots. Their friendship with firefighters began when water pumps and ladder wagons were

pulled by teams of horses. Dalmatians have been called coach dogs and carriage dogs, and even plum pudding dogs because their spots are as dark as plums in white pudding. (Dalmatian puppies are born pure white, and the spots appear as they grow.) Through the years their jobs and names have changed, but today's Dalmatians still look like their chariot-chasing ancestors.

Miniature dogs, such as Pekingese, Pomeranians, and Chihuahuas, come from a long line of runts. At first, small dogs were bred to be lapdogs or "under-the-table" dogs. In the Near East they were called comfort dogs because they could be held across a person's stomach like a heating pad. In China they were called sleeve dogs because they could be carried in the loose sleeve of a kimono.

The dainty Pekingese is an ancient breed from China. Its name comes from the Chinese city of Peking, where many legends are told about the tiny dogs. One story says that when a lioness grew tired of her gruff lion husband, she went to live with a butterfly. Their babies were the Pekingese — forever brave as lions but as dainty as butterflies.

Pekingese dogs lived in palaces. Only the emperor and his family owned them. For centuries, anyone caught stealing a Pekingese was put to death. But in the 1800s, a British soldier smuggled one of the precious dogs out of China. After he gave it to Queen Victoria in England, Pekingese dogs became popular in the Western world, too.

Pekingese, salukis, huskies, Dalmatians, and Afghan

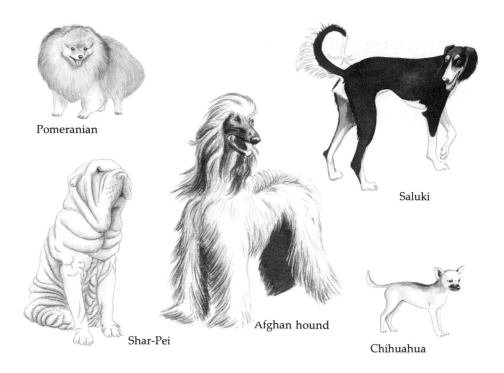

Pomeranian

Saluki

Shar-Pei

Afghan hound

Chihuahua

hounds are very old breeds, but many others are quite new. The Doberman pinscher was created only a hundred years ago in Germany. In 1890, a dog lover named Louis Doberman decided he wanted a new kind of dog — a big dog that would be a strong athlete and a loyal guard. He liked the faithful German shepherds, and he admired the sturdy black guard dogs called Rottweilers. Rottweilers were an old breed of dog brought to Germany by Roman invaders.

Mr. Doberman knew that if he chose a German shepherd parent and a Rottweiler parent, the various puppies would inherit certain traits from the mother and certain traits from the father, in different combinations. And that's what he wanted, a mixture from which he could start a new breed. From each litter, Mr. Doberman selected the puppies that looked most like the dog he had in mind. Finally, in 1910, he had the new short-haired, athletic dogs, which people called "Doberman's dogs." They weren't as sleek as today's Doberman pinschers, but they were as tough as the Rottweilers and as loyal as the German shepherds. Mr. Doberman added the name pinscher, which means terrier. A terrier is a dog "of the earth" that likes to dig into burrows after small animals.

Mr. Doberman could "build" a new dog because all dogs are related. No matter what their size or shape or color, they are the same species. Animals of the same species can mate and

have babies. A Saint Bernard and a golden retriever can be parents together. A dachshund can mate with a fluffy poodle or a hairless Chihuahua. Any combination is possible.

There are fads and fashions in dogs. During the 1930s and 1940s, cocker spaniels were favorite household pets. In the 1950s and 1960s, the sturdy, square-headed boxers were popular. Then poodles became top dogs. Now the dogs people want most are Rottweilers, German shepherds, and Doberman pinschers, especially in crowded cities, where people want guard dogs for protection. Throughout the years, people have loved the easygoing golden retrievers and Labrador retrievers to help in hunting, but also because they are such good friends. But people like unusual dogs, too, such as the tiny Lhasa apso from Tibet, which is easy to keep in an apartment, or the wrinkled Shar-Pei, which looks like its skin is too big for its body.

Around the world there are probably three or four hundred different breeds of dogs, but the American Kennel Club (AKC) lists 130 breeds that are called purebreds. A purebred is a dog whose parents and ancestors are the same breed as far back as anyone knows. But most of the 52 million or more dogs in this country are a mixture of breeds. Some people call them mutts. They are all-purpose dogs that can guard a house, bring in a newspaper, catch a Frisbee, snooze on a kid's bed, or do whatever their owners ask of them.

Life would be far different without dogs. The sheepdogs of New Zealand are so important that a common saying is "No dog, no shepherd. No shepherd, no sheep. No sheep, no wool or meat." Dogs are companions for people who are blind or deaf or confined to wheelchairs. They can lead their friends across busy streets, turn on lights, alert them to visitors, or pick up dropped pencils in school. Dogs rescue people buried by earthquakes, floods, and avalanches. They sniff out drugs and explosives, pull sleds, and entertain us in movies and on television. They are loyal, smart, playful, and hardworking. Many dog owners would swear that their dogs are practically human. Almost all the qualities we love and admire in dogs came from their wolf ancestors, those social animals so much like us.

Dogs were the first animals to serve us. They started the great Age of Domestication, which changed the way human beings

live. Our first best friends herded and captured and helped domesticate other animals that could be used for food or transportation. When people had domestic animals to take care of, they began to settle down and build civilizations.

But then a strange thing happened. Once humans teamed up with dogs, they no longer admired wolves. Wolves became the scary, dangerous bad guys, and the loyal dogs stood guard to keep the wolves away. And ever since, people have been afraid of wolves. We've killed so many and forced so many from their natural habitats that there are few wolves left in the world.

It has been said that "we give dogs love we can spare, time we can spare, and room we can spare. In return, dogs give us their all. It's the best deal man has ever made."

Shouldn't we pay back the favor? It's time to give wolves the room they need, the protection they need, and the respect they deserve as the ancient great-grandparents of our best friends.

2 Who Caught the Cat?

In one of Rudyard Kipling's *Just So Stories*, "The Cat that Walked by Himself," Mr. Kipling tells how Wild Dog became man's First Friend and guarded the cave, Wild Horse became man's first servant to carry man upon his back, and Wild Cow became Giver of Good Food. But the wildest of all animals was the Cat. Cat made a bargain to kill mice and be kind to babies when he is in the house, just as long as the babies don't pull his tail too hard. "But when he has done that . . . he is the Cat that walks by himself, and all places are alike to him."

And that's just the way cats live. A house is a cat's own territory, which it allows humans to share. Cats live a kind of double life. At home they are domesticated animals, content to sleep on soft cushions and eat delicious food. But as soon as they walk out the door, they are once again wild and free, quite able to take care of themselves.

It has been said that cats were the only loners to become

domesticated. All the other animals that went to work for humans live in some kind of social group, such as a pack, a herd, or a flock, that is easily captured. But recently in England, scientists discovered that when many cats live close together, as on a farm, they behave like prides of lions. The female cats feed and take care of one another's kittens, just as female lions do. When a young male lion takes over the leadership of a pride, he kills all the new cubs that were fathered by the old leader. The scientists saw male farm cats do the same thing. We still have a lot to find out about the secret life of cats. It may be that cats came into human households because they like being part of a protected "pride."

Cats became domesticated long after dogs did, after people had stopped wandering and had settled down to raise crops. The hunters of the Stone Age had no use for cats. But when farmers started to store grain, they had a problem only the cats could fix: the first crop robbers were mice and rats.

In Egypt, where the first silo was invented about four thousand years ago, mice and rats swarmed over the grain stored in the silos for cattle. It must have seemed like fast-food heaven to the rodents, but it was even better for cats. No more lying in wait in the grass for some prey to come by. Here was an endless feast of fat, well-fed mice. No wonder the African wildcats stayed close to human settlements, and no wonder the Egyptian people were pleased to have them.

As wolves are the ancestors of dogs, African wildcats are the ancestors of domesticated cats. African wildcats, which still

exist today, look very much like ordinary farm cats. They are small and slender, with long tapered tails and large ears. Some are spotted, some striped, some plain. They range in color from light gray or sandy beige to reddish brown.

Although a few wildcats may have been tamed or kept captive once in a while by other people, it was the Egyptians who first treated cats like royal guests. They even worshiped them as gods. Bastet was a goddess in the shape of a cat. People believed that cats were Bastet's messengers on earth and that a cat's glowing eyes could protect people from harm in the dark of night. Women put makeup around their eyes to make them look like cats' eyes. Cats were everywhere, but the ones that lived in the homes of rich people wore gold necklaces and jewels.

In those days in Egypt, a person could be put to death for killing a cat. Cats were so valuable that if there were a fire in a house, the cat was saved first. And when a cat died, it was wrapped carefully like a mummy and buried in a cat-shaped wooden coffin or a woven basket. Family members shaved their eyebrows as a sign of their sadness. Each spring at a cat temple in the city of Bast, thousands of people gathered to honor the goddess Bastet and the millions of cats buried there.

The Egyptians were so fond of their cats that they wanted to keep them for themselves. No one was allowed to take cats out of the country. Well, as soon as people are told they can't have something, they seem to want it. Soon cats were smuggled aboard trading ships leaving Egypt. It wasn't long before cats lived in many countries, which was a good thing because rats and mice were spreading like wildfire, too. In India, China, and Japan, women wanted cats to keep rats and mice away from precious silkworm cocoons.

But cats weren't always welcomed. Egyptians liked the cat's independent ways, but in other places and times, people saw cats as sneaky and wicked. Things turned bad for cats about eight hundred years ago, during a time called the Middle Ages. Superstition was at an all-time high. The Christian church was growing, and old beliefs were changing. Cats, which had once been worshiped, now were seen as false gods. They were said to live with witches, who kept them as evil messengers of demons.

People came to fear cats, whose eyes glowed in the dark and whose howl could sound almost human. They didn't trust an animal that could appear silently or land on its feet so gracefully without getting hurt. The cat seemed to have nine lives! As superstitions grew, countless numbers of cats were tortured and killed.

During England's chill winters, people wore cloaks made of fur. But in the year 1127, the Catholic church prohibited nuns from wearing expensive furs. They could only use the cheaper fur from rabbits and cats. A lot of cats were killed that year.

On the Isle of Man, off the coast of England, where the islanders are called Manx, there's also a cat called a Manx. It has no tail. The islanders believed their tailless cats were smarter

than any others, but one king of Wales in the Middle Ages wouldn't allow them in his country. He said that all cats must be "perfect of tail." He thought cats without tails were weird — they might join the spooks of night.

Superstitions don't disappear easily, but they can change. On Halloween we still put up decorations of witches and black cats, but now it's just for fun. Even today, some people in Europe and the United States get jumpy when a black cat walks across their path, because they think it's bad luck. In Britain, though, a black cat can mean good luck.

We know now that a cat's eyes glow in the dark because they have an extra layer of cells that acts like a mirror to reflect more light. Cats can't see in total darkness, but, like all night hunters, they see in the dark better than we do because of this extra layer. Cats also find their way around in the dark by sound, smell, and the gentle touch of whiskers. Twenty-four whiskers, twelve on each side of a cat's face, in rows of four, feel the slightest movement of air, and that sends a message to the cat's brain about the size and shape of the object in the cat's way.

Now we know that a cat lands on its feet because it twists in midair with its back arched high to add spring to its stretched-out legs. And a cat appears silently because it walks on softly padded toes. There is no *click, click* on the floor because the cat's sharp, curved claws are pulled back and hidden until it needs them.

Cats were not bred and raised for special work as dogs were. Their biggest job has always been pest control. All breeds of cats are good mousers. For several weeks, someone once counted the mice killed each day by one cat that lived in a stadium. He figured out that this champion mouser had killed 12,480 mice in six years.

Thomas Huxley was only half joking when he declared that the British Empire owed its power to cats. Cats that lived on farms and in rural villages kept down the number of field mice that raided bees' nests, he said. Bees are the only insects that pollinate red clover. So red clover grew abundantly in farm pastures, where cattle fed. With a rich diet of clover, the cattle produced nutritious beef that kept British sailors strong and

Abyssinian

Scottish fold

Sphinx

Persian

healthy. And strong, healthy sailors could guard all the nations belonging to the British Empire around the world — all because cats ate the field mice!

There are a hundred or more different breeds of cats today. Most of them are bred for beauty or just because they are unusual in some way. But most common are the "alley cats," the mixed breeds found everywhere.

The slim Abyssinian cats, with their almond-shaped green or golden eyes, look most like the ancient cats of Egypt. Thousands of years ago they came from the African country of Abyssinia, which is now Ethiopia.

Maine coon

Tabby

Angora

Siamese

One of the oldest of the long-haired cats is the silky Angora, which came from Turkey and got its name from that country's capital city, Ankara. In the 1500s, Angoras were taken to Europe, where wealthy people paid a lot of money to buy them for pets.

Early settlers brought short-haired cats to America in the 1600s because the cats were good mousers. American shorthairs come in many patterns, such as the striped cats we call tabbies and the patchwork cats called calicoes.

Persian cats, with their long silky hair, are popular pets because they love to be pampered. They were bred from some long-haired cats of Persia (which is now Iran) and the fluffy Angora cats of Turkey.

Hundreds of years ago, the dainty blue-eyed Siamese cats guarded the palace of the king of Siam (a country now called Thailand). These smart, athletic cats were trained to pace the palace walls and jump on the backs of anyone trying to break in. Since they came to the United States in 1890, Siamese cats haven't been used as watchcats, but they are lovable, lively pets.

Many people used to think that Maine coon cats were part cat and part racoon, but they're not. They're a cross between the soft Angora and some short-haired cats that came to New England with settlers in the days of the Pilgrims. Coon cats are big and muscular, with shaggy coats.

The Scottish fold cat is a good example of how a new breed comes about. In 1961, a kitten named Susie was born in a litter of farm cats in Scotland. Susie had a mutation: one of her ears was folded down like a little cap. When she grew up, some of her kittens also had folded ears. After that, cats with folded ears were chosen as the parents of new litters in order to continue getting litters of folded-ear cats.

In the 1960s in California, someone bred a very unusual cat called the ragdoll. This cat is so calm and gentle that when anyone picks it up, it hangs with legs dangling, as limp as a ragdoll. But it's such a "cool" cat that it won't even protect itself from a dog or another cat, not even if it's in pain. It will always need an owner's love and protection.

Another strange breed from the 1960s is the sphinx cat from Canada. It's also called the Canadian hairless, and sometimes the moon cat. It has no whiskers, no eyebrows, and no fur except for some downy hair on its face. Cats like the sphinx and the ragdoll probably could not survive on their own. They are so different from the original wildcat that they can only live as domestic animals. These odd breeds seem to have lost the freedom of the Cat that Walked by Himself.

There are 58 million pet cats in America. More money is spent on cat food than on baby food. One of the reasons cats are the number one pet today is their ability to take care of themselves. As long as it has a litter box, food, water, and a cozy place to nap, a cat is content to be left alone while grown-ups go to work and children go to school.

But for all their independence, cats are loyal and brave. Many have protected homes and alerted their families to fires. Each year, the Latham Foundation in California gives medals to animal heroes. Shade McCorkle is a gray-striped cat of no particular breed. He won the foundation's gold medal for protecting his owner, eighty-eight-year-old Nell Mitchell, from a burglar. Shade was napping under a blanket on his owner's bed, when a man broke in and demanded Mrs. Mitchell's money and jewelry. She didn't answer, so the man slapped her. Shade leapt on the burglar with a blood-chilling scream. He slashed the man's face with his teeth and claws. The burglar grabbed the cat and pulled him off. But Shade flung himself at the man again. He clawed and bit with the fury of his African wildcat ancestor. Finally, covered with blood, the man threw Shade against a table and ran out. Shade was badly bruised, but Mrs. Mitchell was safe.

Like Kipling's Cat that Walked by Himself, all cats have kept their bargain with people. They are both domestic and wild at the same time. Someone has said that God made the cat only to give people the pleasure of petting the tiger.

Who caught the cat? Probably no one. Cats invited themselves into our households, but they are more than guests. Like dogs, they've become part of the family.

3

Who Harnessed the Horse?

One warm September afternoon in 1940, four boys headed for the steep, rugged cliffs near their village in the south of France. They circled around "Donkey's Hole," a small crevice in a pasture, into which a donkey had vanished some years before. As they got near a slope called Lascaux, the oldest boy whistled for his small terrier, but the dog didn't come running. After an hour of calling, the boy told his friends he was going back to Donkey's Hole. And there, when he yelled down into the narrow dark tunnel, his dog's bark echoed from far below.

The dog couldn't get out of the hole, so the boys scrambled in after it. They found themselves in a cave no one had seen for thousands of years. The next day they went back to Donkey's Hole with ropes and lights to explore further. And that's when they discovered the Great Hall of Bulls. It is an enormous room that opens into several steep galleries where the rock walls are covered with paintings. Wild bulls, larger than life,

run with horses and deer. Each animal was drawn in thick black lines, with the details of muscles, hooves, and fur painted in white, brown, red, and yellow, so bright they look fresh and new.

The beautiful paintings in the Lascaux caves were created by artists who lived about thirty thousand years ago. Stone Age people used the caves as a place to celebrate success in hunting. It may have been a place of magic and ceremony, as sacred to them as our churches and temples are to us.

The horse painted on those cave walls was a small, sturdy, reddish brown animal with black legs and a mane that grew in a thick short brush, as though it had been clipped. This "caveman's pony" is the grandfather of all the horses we know today. It is called Przewalski's horse, named after a Russian explorer. Nikolai Przewalski wanted to be the first European to enter the forbidden city of Lhasa in Tibet. He never got there, but on several expeditions he collected nine hundred different plants and several animals that had not been seen in Europe before. On his last trip, in 1885, across the Gobi desert of Mongolia, he saw herds of wild horses that galloped away before he could catch up with them. But he bought the skull and skin of one of these horses and took them back to a Russian museum. Today these horses are extinct in the wild, but a few are alive and well in zoos.

Przewalski's horse, and a close cousin called the tarpan, ran in herds all across Europe and Asia, from the flat frozen tundra to forests and warm seacoasts. Like the other animals painted

Przewalski's horse

on the cave walls, wild horses were hunted for meat and skins. Stone Age people probably kept a few horses penned up so they'd be right on hand for meat. Their dogs would have helped them run herds of wild horses through narrow ravines into dead-end canyons or gullies that could be closed off like corrals. Horses are easier to take care of than cattle or sheep, which have to be fed in the winter. Horses can fend for themselves. Even in the coldest weather they can scrape away snow with their hooves and find food.

No one knows exactly when people began to use horses for more than food and clothing. Maybe a colt was left behind in a stampede or separated from the herd. A young horse would have been easy to tame and raise. The person who stayed on a horse's back for the first time could never have guessed how he changed civilization. Dogs gave humans friendship, but horses gave humans speed and power. Horses have been called "the proudest conquest of Man."

The first riders rode bareback. There were no saddles, no harnesses, no bridles or bits. A rider hung onto the horse's mane and had little control. But a runaway animal doesn't stop just because you yank on its mane. So next came the idea of putting a rope or leather thong around the horse's neck. But if a rider pulled on the rope too hard, the horse could choke. What would get the horse's attention fast enough to make it stop when the rider wanted? Some clever person invented a gadget called a bit, which fits in the space between the horse's front teeth and its back molars. The first bit was made from

bone or antlers. It was tied to the reins so that it bit into the animal's tender lips when the rider pulled hard. It didn't take a horse long to learn to stop when it felt a tug on the reins.

Archeologists once believed that horses pulled carts and chariots long before anyone rode horseback. Until fairly recently, the earliest evidence of horseback riding was a 2,500-year-old metal bit found in the ancient city of Athens in Greece. Other artifacts showed that horses had been used to pull chariots much longer — since 2000 B.C. (which means before the birth of Christ). But more than twenty years ago, Soviet scientists found some objects that dated from 3000 or 4000 B.C.: a small carved horse-head figure with a bridle on it, as well as pieces of a reindeer antler that looked as though they had been used as a bit for a horse's mouth.

Two archeologists from the United States, Dr. David Anthony and Dorcas Brown, were intrigued by the Soviet scientists' discovery. It seemed to them that it would have been easier to learn to ride a horse than to invent the wheel and the chariot. They learned that they could tell whether a horse had been ridden by checking its teeth. When a horse bites down on a bit, the bit leaves a mark on its teeth. Dr. Anthony and Ms. Brown studied the teeth of four thousand horses that had been buried for thousands of years. Finally, in a museum in the city of Kiev in the Ukraine, they found what they were looking for — a tooth with the marks made by a bit. That horse had been ridden. It was six thousand years old.

Does it matter if we know when horses were ridden? Archeologists say yes. Horseback riding changed the way people lived. It meant they could move faster and farther. It changed the way they fought their enemies, how they traded, and where they settled.

The invention of saddles and stirrups made a big difference in the way people rode. One of the first saddles perched on the horse's back the way a camel's saddle does, with no stirrups for the feet. Gradually saddle designs changed to suit the rider's purpose. By medieval times, when knights rode forth in shining armor, a saddle was a deep seat that could hold a man wearing a four-hundred-pound metal suit. Today, cowboys, who spend days on horseback, need a comfortable saddle with a handy horn on it to anchor a rope. Jockeys use the smallest

saddles possible so their racehorses aren't slowed down by extra weight.

Soldiers on horseback could overtake foot soldiers easily. Back in the thirteenth century, the Mongols of Central Asia were fierce fighters. They invented stirrups so they could stand as they charged the enemy with spears or sharp, curved scimitars. Most of the soldiers in the armies of ancient Greece and Rome didn't need horses, because most of their battles defended walled cities. But their generals and officers rode horseback. A beautiful well-trained horse was as much a symbol of power then as an expensive car is to some people today. A man considered it an honor to sacrifice a pure white stallion to the gods of ancient Greece. And today, riders still follow the basic instructions for riding that were written in Greece 2,400 years ago.

William the Conqueror invaded England with knights on horseback in 1066. After that, the English began to breed powerful war-horses that could carry a man in full armor. But by the 1300s, when armies began to use guns, they no longer needed huge war-horses. They wanted lighter, faster animals. Some of the best came from Arabia.

The Arabians became famous for breeding intelligent horses with sleek coats and strong, slender bodies. When the English knights traveled to the Middle East during the Crusades, they took some of the Arabian horses back to England. The Arabians were bred with English horses to develop the racehorses known as Thoroughbreds.

The dog-size prehistoric ancestor of the horse once lived on the North American continent, but it became extinct millions of years before any humans lived here. The first modern horse set foot in North America in 1519, when Hernando Cortés brought eleven stallions, five mares, and one foal that was born on board his ship from Spain. The Native Americans were amazed at these big "sky dogs" that ran like the wind. Spanish explorers were claiming land as fast as they could, and in 1540, Francisco Coronado moved north into New Mexico with 245 horses. He was searching for gold, but he found the Grand Canyon. He kept going across what is now Texas, then through Oklahoma and into Kansas. Along the way, some of his horses strayed.

Those strays, which returned to the wild, were the ancestors of the wild mustangs that still roam the West today. At one time there were two million or more of these *feral* mustangs, but now there are only twenty thousand or so. Their ranges have been pushed back by cattle ranchers who want more grazing land, and thousands of the mustangs have been turned into dog food. By the 1600s, the western Plains Indians had captured enough of the feral horses to begin a breed that would suit their life on the open plains. They needed a swift, sturdy horse, and that's what they created in the Indian pony or Appaloosa.

The wild ponies of Chincoteague Island, Virginia, are feral. Their ancestors were aboard Spanish ships on their way to the New World when the ships went down in a terrible storm.

Arabian

Thoroughbred

Clydesdales

Some of the ponies swam to safety on the island, and ponies
have been there ever since. Horses went to Australia with the
first European settlers in the 1700s. Some of those horses
strayed, and their feral descendants are called brambies.

When our country was new, the owners of huge tobacco
plantations in Maryland and Virginia took pride in their "walking horses." From horseback, an owner could easily check the
fields and watch his slaves. For fun, the owners raced their

Walking horse

Appaloosa

Quarter horse

horses along a quarter-mile stretch of road. Horses good at quick starts for these short sprints were called quarter horses. A Thoroughbred named Janus, which arrived in Virginia in 1756 from England, is the ancestor of many of today's champion American quarter horses.

Dutch settlers brought heavy workhorses for the farms in the Northeast. These became the Clydesdales, Percherons, shires, and Belgian draft horses once used to plow and harvest or to pull the huge wagons to market. Most of them have been replaced by tractors and trucks, so now many of them only wear their fancy harnesses to parade at county fairs.

Horses and oxen helped pioneers open the American western frontier. Oxen pulled covered wagons, and horses carried the mail and pulled stagecoaches. Riders for the pony express carried the mail from Saint Joseph, Missouri, to Sacramento, California. It took about ten days to cover the 1,800-mile route, stopping at 157 stations along the way. Six or eight times between stations, a rider would change horses. He'd leap off his tired horse and onto a fresh mount that was saddled and ready to go. The pony express system was only in business from August 1860 to October 1861. The development of the first coast-to-coast telegraph system made the pony express unnecessary.

The Wells Fargo company kept stagecoaches going with teams of fresh horses waiting at stations along the rugged route from Missouri to the West Coast. The company started as a

bank for handling gold during the California Gold Rush, but it branched out into passenger service in 1855. After the first cross-country railroad was finished in 1869, the stagecoaches gradually went out of business.

But horses were still necessary, even in cities. Before the invention of trucks and motorcars, every carriage, streetcar, ambulance, fire pump, and hearse was horse drawn. Milk, bread, and ice were delivered house to house by horse-drawn wagons. The delivery horses knew the routes by heart and didn't need the driver's hand on the reins. They stopped and started, stopped and started, dozens of times each day. After a milkman had delivered milk and cream to a house, the horse would move on to stop at the next customer's house almost automatically.

There was a horse for every occasion, or so it seemed, but a horse is almost a luxury now.

Owning Thoroughbred racehorses is more than luxury. It is big business. One of the most famous racers was Secretariat,

the first horse in twenty-five years to win three of the biggest races for the Triple Crown. Secretariat retired to a stud farm after he'd raced for only sixteen months. The fees paid for Secretariat's service to father more than three hundred offspring earned his owner more than six million dollars.

Racing was a growing sport in America until 1802, when all racetracks in the Northeast closed because some religious groups didn't think anyone should bet on fast horses. After that, harness racing became popular. In this sport, a pacing horse or trotting horse pulls a rider seated on a small cart called a sulky. Some people in the same religious groups that had objected to racing argued that a trotting horse wasn't really racing because it wasn't going as fast as it really could. Today, the racetracks are open again, betting is permitted, and harness racing is still popular, too.

The Amish people still depend on horse-drawn vehicles, and we still honor the horse when we describe the strength of a car engine in horsepower. A few city police still oversee parades and traffic from the backs of their well-groomed horses. But soldiers no longer fight on horseback. Mounted soldiers are honor guards for celebrations and great occasions. The riderless horse, with boots placed backward in its stirrups, represents the fallen hero. When President John F. Kennedy was killed, a black riderless horse was led to the burial site at Arlington National Cemetery.

But when the civil rights hero Martin Luther King, Jr., was buried, his body was carried to the cemetery in a wagon drawn

Donkey Horse Mule

by mules. His honor guard reminded people of Dr. King's slave ancestors, who worked with mules while their owners rode fine horses. Mules were not domesticated from wild animals. They were deliberately created by humans from a cross between a horse and the good old reliable, sturdy donkey, which carried people on its back long before anyone rode horseback.

More than six thousand years ago, wandering people hunted the small wild donkeys of North Africa for meat. In China and the Middle East, donkey skin was used to make a fine paperlike parchment to write on. It was in the valley of the great Nile River in Egypt that donkeys were domesticated.

When the Spaniards conquered South America in the 1500s, they took donkeys with them as work animals. Donkeys were surefooted in the high Andes Mountains, and they have worked there ever since. There is hardly a place on earth — except perhaps the cold polar regions — without donkeys.

They work everywhere, from pulling carts in coal and diamond mines to carrying tourists up and down the steep walls of the Grand Canyon.

Donkeys will carry heavy loads and work long hours, but they have a reputation for being stubborn. They balk when they've had enough or when they are badly treated.

Mules are hard workers, too. Mule owners argue that their mules are smarter and stronger than horses or donkeys. And that may be, because mules have a chance to carry the best traits of both horses and donkeys. A mule's mother is a horse, with a donkey as the father. The first donkeys and horses may have crossed accidently. Donkeys and horses grazed together, and somewhere along the line, they mated. Mules are mentioned in the Bible, which means they've been around for at least two thousand years. In this country, mules were bred to work in the cotton fields of Mississippi, the plantations of Louisiana, and the coal mines of West Virginia.

Each time a farmer wants a mule foal, he must bring together a female horse and a male donkey, which is also called a jackass. Although horses and donkeys are related, they are different species. Lions and tigers, for example, are both cats, but they are different species. If a lion and tiger mate, their baby is a tiglon. But a tiglon is the end of the line. It is *sterile*. It can't produce any young like itself. So it is with mules.

If any animal is a symbol of domestication, it is certainly the mule. Maybe it should be called "the proudest production of Man."

4 Who Got the Goat?

Thousands of reindeer rumble like thunder down a steep Arctic slope. As closely packed as a flock of sheep, the herd trots across the frozen ground, their hooves clacking like cracked knuckles. Their long antlers bob and weave like bare branches in a breeze. Whenever a few reindeer veer away, two small black dogs race after them and nip at their legs until they join the herd again. One Laplander skis ahead of the herd, and two skiers follow behind. The herdsmen have come from their base camp one hundred miles north of the Arctic Circle. They have more modern skis than the herdsmen who worked a thousand years ago, but otherwise, their jobs are very much the same.

In the Arctic region called Lapland, reindeer do the work of goats, sheep, cows, and horses combined. Lapland isn't a country itself. It's made up of the northern edges of Sweden, Norway, Finland, and the Soviet Union. It's a tough place for people to live. The sun doesn't rise for two months of the nine-month winter. It doesn't set for two months in the summer. But reindeer thrive in this bleak, frozen land.

A reindeer is no taller than a pony. Its wide feet, spread out like snowshoes, and the two claw-shaped bumps behind its hooves keep it from sinking into swamps or snowdrifts. The clicking noise of the feet is made by the movement of ligaments. A reindeer carries its big head low, like a moose. Both the males and females have long, branched antlers. Antlers aren't hollow and permanent like horns. They are solid, and they fall off each year, which is handy because people don't have to kill a reindeer in order to use the antlers. One section of the antler grows low over the reindeer's face and protects its nose and skull like a shield.

Reindeer move by the seasons. The females go first to the calving grounds, where their babies are born each spring. A few days later, the males follow. Nothing stops them. They can swim raging rivers and walk on ice. Reindeer migrate farther than any other land mammal. In herds of twenty thousand or more, the North American reindeer called caribou make a round trip of 1,400 miles each year. They go south from the tundra of the Arctic Circle to the edge of Canadian forests in autumn and back again in spring. They browse on leaves in the forests, lichens on the frozen tundra, and seaweed at the coast of the Arctic Ocean. They have followed the same pattern for thousands of years. Humans couldn't change the migration, so they went with it.

The *Ice Age*, when glaciers covered much of Europe, is also known as the Age of Reindeer. One hundred twenty-one of the pictures painted on the cave walls of France during that time show reindeer. People ate reindeer meat and used the skins for weatherproof clothes and tents. They carved beautiful designs on knives, tools, and jewelry made from the antlers. Hunters often made themselves into decoys. A man wearing the skin and antlers of a reindeer could crawl close to a herd, in the same way that the American Plains Indians disguised themselves when hunting bison. If a hunter killed a female reindeer, he could capture her calf and raise it. Or he could put out salt, which the animals crave, or lure them with extra food. Gradually people tamed a few reindeer.

When the climate warmed and the ice sheets melted back, the reindeer retreated to the north. The people of the northern lands learned to train reindeer to wear harnesses and pull sleighs. They drank reindeer milk and made cheese and butter from it. They do the same today. One Lapp guide, who takes tourists on reindeer-drawn sleigh rides, said, "As you use beef, we use reindeer meat. It's our steak and hamburger."

Billboards in Norway advertise reindeer meat as "the noble taste of the wild." But, says one report, there is "nothing particularly noble about reindeer herding in the Arctic areas of Norway these days." Times are changing. Herders still drive all the reindeer to one area at breeding time, and owners find their own animals by checking the ear notches that mark their herd. But many of the herders, in a rush to get their animals to

market, now push the reindeer by snowmobile and helicopter. Animals collapse from exhaustion, and veterinarians say that stress is causing the reindeer to get ulcers. They are weakened and fall prey to parasites and disease.

When the herds of North American caribou showed signs of dying out in 1891, the American government decided to bring in tame reindeer from Siberia. They were shipped to Alaska, along with a few herdsmen from Lapland to help train the Eskimos to handle the new herd. By 1940, the herds in Alaska had grown to 250,000, but ten years later only 25,000 were left. Some people blamed wolves. Some reindeer wandered off with local caribou that were migrating by. And some say the decrease in the number of reindeer was due to lack of interest on the part of Eskimos who didn't want to go back to the life of wandering herdsmen again.

About that same time, officials in Michigan decided that reindeer ought to live in the Upper Peninsula of their state, close to the Canadian border. They offered to buy the Alaskan herd, but the price was six hundred dollars for each reindeer. That was too expensive. Instead, Michigan bought sixty reindeer from Norway and hired two Lapp herdsmen to come along. Within five years, the reindeer were gone, except for one old cow who was given a home in the Bell Isle Zoo.

Although reindeer were used as domestic animals for thousands of years, they changed very little. Some were used for milk and others for meat, but even so, they do not come in a wide variety of sizes or colors. Reindeer didn't have to change to suit peoples' needs because people changed their lives to adjust to the animals' habits.

Sheep and goats, on the other hand, have changed greatly since they were first domesticated at about the same time as the reindeer. There are several kinds of mountain goats, such as ibexes and markhors, but the ancestor of domestic goats is a species known officially as the wild goat. These goats live in the Greek islands and in a region that is now Iran and Iraq. They have huge, tough, curved horns, and the males have small beards. A man's small pointed beard is called a goatee because it looks like the goat's.

Goats' hooves are built for climbing. They leap up and down steep, rugged cliffs so fast that it seems as though their feet have suction cups. In a way, they do. The bottom of each hoof curves up, and it is surrounded by a sharp edge, which fits tightly to almost any surface. It wasn't easy for hunters to stalk a goat up steep rock ledges. But they could chase a group of wild goats to the edge of a cliff, knowing that at least one might fall to its death in the valley below. Horses, bison, and many other animals were caught in this way before guns were invented.

The real domestication of goats began about nine thousand years ago. People found that goats follow a leader and that a small herd could be kept moving with the help of a dog. When a tribe camped at a water hole, a few herdsmen could prevent the goats from wandering too far. Goats have been called the "poor man's cow," because they give rich milk but they don't need large pastures, as cows do. In cartoons, goats eat every-thing from tin cans to shoes, but in real life, goats are more particular. They browse on shrubs, and they even leap onto low tree branches to reach the tenderest leaves. Archeologists say that about eight thousand years ago, the newly domesti-cated goats in some regions destroyed so many trees and shrubs that people were left without wood for fuel. And that forced people to keep moving instead of settling down.

In the early days of civilization, goats were kept on hand for ceremonies and sacrifices. Imagine living at a time when the total darkening of the sun during an eclipse, for example, might have been seen as punishment from an angry god. But if people killed an animal and did not eat it or use any part of it, the gods who controlled their lives might accept this sacrifice as a gift. A happy god would send rain instead of drought, good crops instead of none, good health instead of sickness.

Not all the goats were used for sacrifice, of course. Five thou-sand years ago, the Egyptians tanned goatskin for leather, as we know from the still-soft pieces recently discovered inside the pyramids. Goatskin canteens are still used by hikers, skiers, and shepherds to carry wine or water. Horns and bones were turned into knives, tools, cups, and jewelry.

Goats became known as walking drugstores. Their blood was said to cure callouses on a person's feet, and people wore rings made from goat horn to protect them from illness. But the real prize from a goat were the bezoars, or stomach stones. These are round, tightly packed balls of hair. When a goat licks its body, it swallows loose hair, which collects in its stomach. Bezoars aren't digested. They stay in the goat's stomach, where they get churned around until they are smooth and hard as rock. Even now, some people still believe that stomach stones can cure cancer and other diseases.

Goats took kindly to domestication. They can be as friendly as dogs, and they like to follow people around. One or two goats can keep a family in milk and cheese. Wherever people settled, goats went with them. Goats were small and tough enough for ocean voyages, and it wasn't long before they had spread around the world. Captain Cook took the first goats to Hawaii in 1778. But two Hawaiian chiefs argued over who should have the goats. They couldn't decide, so they killed them. A few years later, Captain Vancouver brought more goats. Some of the *descendants* of that second batch of goats have gone wild. These feral goats have just about wiped out several of Hawaii's native plants. No browsing or grazing animals had ever lived on the islands, so the native plants never developed any defenses, such as spines or thorns or poisonous leaves.

The same thing happened in the Galápagos Islands. One male and two female goats were left on Pinta Island in 1959. Since they had no natural enemies on the island, the goats thrived. By 1973, there were thirty thousand goats, and the conservation department urged hunters to shoot them. The island of Santiago still has about a hundred thousand goats munching and killing plants and trampling on tortoise eggs.

Dozens of different breeds of domestic goats are raised in almost every country. They are smaller than their wild ancestors, without the huge curved horns. They pull carts and provide milk, cheese, skins, and wool. The most famous for its milk is the white Saanen goat from the Swiss Alps. Another good milker is the droopy-eared Nubian goat from Africa, which can give four to six quarts of milk each day.

People who like to wear soft cashmere coats and sweaters can thank the goats that come from Tibet and India. Cashmere wool is expensive because one goat can supply only three ounces of the soft, downy fleece. Another strong, smooth wool

is called mohair. It's woven from the silky fleece that lies underneath the long curly hair of Angora goats. (But Angora *wool* doesn't come from these goats. That comes from a rabbit.)

Hunters say, "A hair lost by a hunter is heard by a deer, smelled by a boar, and seen by the mouflon ram." Keen eyesight helps the wild mouflon sheep survive on high, rocky slopes on the islands of Corsica and Sardinia, where their lambs are threatened by hawks and eagles. Each spring, the mountains ring with the clash of rams' horns as two males fight for leadership. These tough mouflon sheep are the ancestors of domestic sheep, and two animals could hardly be more different.

Sheep were not domesticated for their wool. Wild sheep didn't have thick coats of woolly fleece. They were brown, hairy animals — never white. Their warm, waterproof layer of wool was like insulated underwear, beneath a long stringy topcoat. But long before people used wool, they ate the good meat, called mutton. They used the hard fat, called tallow, to make candles and soap, and the horns for cups and trophies.

If you looked at a strand of wool under a microscope, you'd see that it is scaly. These scales are what keep wool clumped together. Once a year wild sheep molt, or shed their coats. As sheep browse, clumps of their molting hair and wool get caught in brambles and thorny branches. Way back in the Stone Age, people knew how to make rope and twine from vines and plant fibers. But it must have been a nice surprise when people found that these dirty brown clumps of soft stuff stuck together. And when it was patted and pulled, it stuck together even more. It "felted." Felt cloth is made from matted fur or wool. Raw wool right off the sheep is waterproof. There's so much oil, called lanolin, in the raw wool that water runs right off a sheep's back. Perhaps people first used the woolly clumps to make soft, waterproof linings for a baby's sleeping place, or as padding to tuck into their foot coverings for more warmth.

It may have been the chance appearance of some lambs whose woolly undercoats outgrew their hairy topcoats that gave people the idea of trying to select and breed these animals for wool. Today's sheep have changed so much that their ancient ancestors wouldn't recognize them. They come in all sizes, with and without horns, and with and without wool.

There are more than two hundred different breeds of sheep, divided into three categories: long-wool sheep, which provide tough fiber for carpets; medium-wool sheep, which are used for meat as well as wool; and fine-wool sheep, which give the soft wool used for clothing.

Lincoln sheep, brought to America from England in 1780, are a long-wool breed. Karakul sheep also have coarse, wiry brown or black wool that is made into carpeting, but the lambs have such soft curly fleece that their pelts are sold as broadtail or Persian lamb for making fur coats.

Hampshires, Shropshires, and Southdowns are some of the medium-wool sheep also sold for meat, and the merino is one of the most famous of the fine-wool sheep. For centuries Spain protected its thick-coated, fleecy merino sheep and wouldn't

Mouflon

Lincoln

Hampshire

allow any to leave the country. But in 1801 a few were imported to America, where this sturdy breed can survive even in rough pastures that offer little shelter or water.

Domestic sheep don't shed their wool in spring as their ancestors did. They have to be sheared. It has been said that necessity is the mother of invention. As sheep were bred for thicker, better wool, someone invented shears for clipping it off. Other inventors came up with better ways to spin the raw wool into thread and bigger, faster looms to weave the thread into cloth. Factories began to turn out millions of yards of warm cloth, and that made it possible for more people to live in cold climates. None of this would have happened without the domestic sheep.

Wild mouflon sheep leap from one rocky cliff to another, out of reach of humans. They are a symbol of freedom. Domestic sheep seem just the opposite. They go wherever they are led — to pastures, through baths of sheep-dip to kill parasites, to the shearing sheds, and to slaughter. But they have also led us to a more comfortable life.

5
Who Corralled the Cow?

What was the world's first vending machine?

The cow, because you put grass in one end and milk comes out the udder.

More than 11 million cows show up for work every day in America — no vacations. And every day is the same. Cows spend about six hours eating and eight hours chewing their cuds. They take two breaks for milking time, one in the morning and one at night. A cow drinks an average of 20 gallons of water each day and eats about 40 pounds of corn silage, hay, and grain pellets with extra vitamins. In return, a cow will give an average 14,241 pounds of milk in a year.

Cows didn't always lead such boring lives. The ancient granddaddy of the cattle was the aurochs, which lived thousands of years ago. This member of the wild ox family was a huge beast with long curved horns, like those painted on the walls of the Lascaux caves. If a six-foot-tall man had stood next to an aurochs, he'd only just have been able to see over the animal's shoulder. But only a very brave man would have gotten that close. An aurochs wasn't the kind of animal that would stand still for milking. For thousands of years, the wanderers and gatherers hunted aurochs so they could use the meat, skin, bones, and horns. The aurochs is extinct, but we know a lot about it because the last one lived in an animal preserve in Poland until 1627.

After people settled down and began to farm, aurochs became crop robbers. They trampled over gardens and stomped plants into mush. Imagine people chasing these animals away until someone said something like, "Listen, if these aurochs are going to hang around, we might as well put a fence around them and keep them here." It probably wasn't that easy, of course, but like other herd animals, cattle can be controlled.

Cows must have invented the game of follow the leader. Farmers say that when one cow decides she's hungry and heads for a far corner of the pasture, all the cows follow her, no matter how important she is in the herd. But it's the dominant or lead cow who gets the best food, the coolest place in the shade of a tree, and the first drink of water. In Switzerland, where cows are led from their winter barns to the mountain meadows in spring, the cows fight to decide who'll be the leader. The cow fights are so much fun to watch that farmers in the Swiss canton of Valais take their best lead cows to a contest before they head for pasture. The cow contestants belong to an ancient breed called Herens. They are small, black, and aggressive. People cheer and clap as the animals push and shove each other until one is declared queen of the lead cows and takes home her prize of a shiny new cow bell.

Wild aurochs probably fought for the position of lead cow, too. So if the lead aurochs was captured, others in the herd would follow. Or if an aurochs cow was killed, it would have been easy for the hunter to keep her calf and feed it until the family needed meat.

With the keeping of domestic animals there's a lot of give and take. When they penned the aurochs, people took advantage of having food right at hand. But in return, they had to give their animals food and protection. And they had to clean up after them. Even that had its trade-off. Cattle dung doesn't have an odor once it has dried. Disks of dried dung, also called cow chips, are a good source of fuel when firewood is scarce. As pioneers moved west across the treeless plains of America, they burned cow chips and buffalo chips, as the Native Americans did. In regions of Africa where long years of drought have killed trees, people still collect dung to fuel their fires.

Aurochs were not the only kind of wild oxen to be domesticated. Seven or eight thousand years ago in Tibet, the wild yak was tamed. It's a rugged animal well suited, with its dense coat of wool, to the cold temperatures of the Himalaya Mountains. Yaks are excellent pack animals, but they give milk that is richer than a cow's, and their wool is woven into blankets, coats, tent covers, and rope. Tibet is a land of few trees, so even the yak's manure is valuable for fuel.

Water buffalo

Another of the wild oxen is the water buffalo, which was domesticated in India and Indonesia, where it has worked in the rice paddies for thousands of years. These big, broad-backed animals can pull plows, haul bulky bundles of wood from forests, and till the flooded rice fields. They are such gentle animals that young children can easily control them. It's a perfect partnership because the water buffalo loves to submerge itself in water to cool off.

Like their oxen cousins, the first tamed aurochs carried heavy

loads or were hitched up to drag plows or carts. It didn't take people long to figure out that smaller cattle would be easier to handle than the huge aurochs-size animals. They selected and mated smaller cows with smaller bulls. New breeds of cattle were created to fit different needs. Milking came thousands of years later, although no one knows exactly when. A wild cow makes only enough milk to feed her calf. As soon as the calf is old enough to eat grass, the cow's milk stops. But farmers found ways to make a cow produce more milk. When a cow has just had a calf, she is said to freshen with new milk, so farmers made sure their cows had calves often. They coaxed or weaned calves away from their mothers' milk much sooner than a calf would usually stop nursing. Then if the farmer continued to milk the cow, the milk kept flowing.

In the ruins of the ancient city of Babylon, near today's city of Baghdad, archeologists found a six-thousand-year-old panel carved in stone. It shows people milking aurochs-like cows, so they must have used the milk. But milk is warm when it comes out of the udder. If it's not used right away or not kept cool, it soon goes sour. There was no ice in Babylon. Milk might have stayed fresh for a day or two in jugs stored in the cool water of a well. But how could they keep all that good milk from going to waste? They made cheese.

An old legend tells of an Arab merchant who carried a water pouch made from the stomach of a sheep. One day, instead of filling it with water, he filled it with milk. After he had traveled all day in the hot desert, he opened the pouch to have a drink.

But the milk had separated into curds and whey. When Little Miss Muffet sat on a tuffet (a cushion), eating her curds and whey, she was eating the lumpy clumps, or curds, that separate from the liquid, called whey. When the whey is poured off, what's left is fresh cheese.

Whether it was by accident or not, cheese making started in the Middle East and spread through Europe. There are hundreds of varieties of cheese made from cow's milk, as well as from the milk of goats, sheep, water buffalo, yak, and llamas.

Thick cream rises to the top of milk. In the days before World War II, when milk was delivered to doorsteps in glass bottles, frozen chunks of icy cream, rising up, sometimes popped cardboard covers right off the bottle tops. Even in ancient times, people knew how to scoop the rich cream from milk and shake or churn it into butter. Scrolls and tablets from ancient Greece and Rome say that butter was used for medicine, especially as a salve to soothe burns. Even now, some people cover a burn with butter if they have no other medicine on hand. Butter from the Asian water buffalo is more solid than cow's butter and less likely to turn rancid in the tropical heat. But it would take some getting used to because it is greenish white. More than 3,500 years ago, Hindus rated their cows by the amount of butter that could be made from their milk, and that is what farmers still do today.

There are forty or fifty different breeds of cattle in this country now, but there were no native American cattle. The first cows sailed to North America in 1611 with the people who settled the colony at Jamestown, Virginia. The next small herd of cows was shipped to the Plimoth colony in Massachusetts in 1624. In these northern colonies, cows found good grazing fields in the summer. But for winter, cows needed hay. Each cow required forty pounds of hay per day, which amounted to four thousand pounds, or two tons, for each animal for the winter. If he had ten cows, a farmer needed to harvest twenty acres of hay each year, which would take him twenty days. But in exchange, he got milk, butter, cheese, meat, hide for leather, and felt. He got horns to use for cups and other containers, tallow for candles and soap, hooves to melt down for glue and gelatin, and intestines to make into casings for sausage.

Two hundred years later, cows trudged west, tied to the covered wagons of the pioneers. Each family needed at least one cow to help them survive in their new settlements. When winter blizzards swept across the prairies, the lucky families were those that had a cow in an attached shed or even in the sod hut with them. Buried under snowdrifts for weeks at a time, they not only had milk but the comfort and warmth of a gentle cow, calmly chewing her cud.

Christopher Columbus brought the first small, black longhorn cattle to the West Indies on his second trip to the New World. On his way to Mexico, the Spanish explorer Hernando Cortés stopped at the West Indies and took calves of those longhorn cattle with him. In 1540, another Spanish explorer, Francisco Coronado, took five hundred head of longhorn cattle to the southwest region of America. Many of the cattle escaped, but they survived in the wild because they were hardy, independent, and fast. With their long horns, which measured six feet across from tip to tip, they could sweep away thorny bushes that hid tufts of grass on the dry ground. They could fight off wolves and hook down clumps of juicy mistletoe that hung from tree branches.

One historian said that longhorns "made more history than any other breed of cattle the civilized world has known." The great open plains of the West became endless pasture for enormous herds of beef cattle, and fortunes were made. Men who owned thousands of cattle were called cattle barons. When the cattle were fat enough to sell, cowboys rounded them up and herded them eastward. The most famous route was the Chisholm Trail. It started south of San Antonio, Texas, and went

across Oklahoma to Abilene, Kansas, where the railroad began. In 1884, cowboys drove more than five million longhorns from Texas to Abilene, where the cattle were loaded into railroad cars that took them to stockyards in the East. Sometimes the river of cattle would be backed up along the trail for forty miles. It's been called the greatest controlled migration of animals in the world.

But by 1920, longhorns were almost extinct because ranchers weren't raising them anymore. The meat industry wanted animals that, as one farmer said, had "to be as uniform in age, color, and conformity as a flock of lambs." With longhorns, it was more likely that no two looked alike. They are big, rangy, long-legged animals that can be black, white, brown, or spotted with slate blue, yellow, or shades of red.

In 1927, the U.S. Forest Service searched for purebred long-horns. They found only thirty purebreds out of millions of other cattle. But longhorns have been saved from extinction by a group of Texas ranchers who are once more breeding these sturdy cattle. They are convinced that the beef industry needs the longhorns because these cattle are resistant to most diseases and parasites and they can thrive on almost dry pastureland.

One of the breeds that took over from the longhorn was the Hereford, a chestnut-colored beef cattle with a white face and white "stockings." The American statesman Henry Clay brought the Hereford to America in 1817 from England, and it immediately became a favorite of beef farmers. Another famous breed is the black Aberdeen Angus cattle from Scotland. There are dozens of other breeds of beef cattle, including the Hays Converter, which is known for its lean meat. The Hays Converter was developed in the last twenty years in Canada from a mixture of Hereford, Holstein, and Brown Swiss cattle.

There are dozens of breeds of milk cattle, too. Six of the most important milk cows in this country are the Ayrshire (AIR-shear), Brown Swiss, Guernsey (GURN-zee), Holstein (some say HOLE-*steen;* others call it HOLE-*stine*), Jersey, and the Milking Shorthorn.

Long ago, when people were still hunters and gatherers, they figured out how to keep meat from spoiling. They dried it, pickled it, or smoked it. People who lived in northern lands could freeze it outdoors. But when people began to use milk, that was another matter. Some leftover milk could be made into

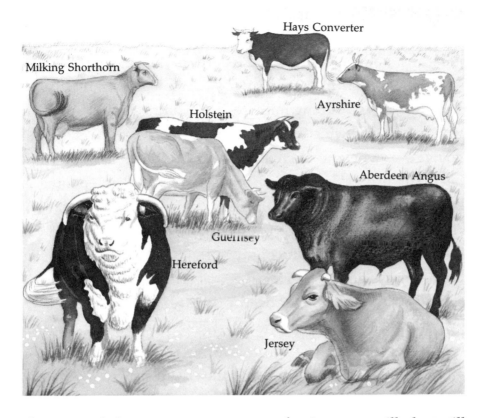

Hays Converter

Milking Shorthorn

Holstein

Ayrshire

Aberdeen Angus

Guernsey

Hereford

Jersey

cheese, and there were some ways of using sour milk, but still a lot of milk went to waste. Even thousands of years later, with icehouses or iceboxes or refrigerators, milk could be kept for only a few days.

Some seasick cows led Louis Borden to come up with a way to keep milk fresh and safe to drink for many weeks. In 1851, he was on his way back to the United States from London on an ocean liner. The sea was so rough that many of the passengers got seasick. The cows in the hold got so sick they couldn't be milked. The babies on board the ship cried so long for milk that Mr. Borden was upset. For five years he tried to figure out a way to preserve milk. Finally he added sugar to it and sealed it in cans. Today people still like Borden's sweetened milk.

Not long after that, in the 1860s, Louis Pasteur announced his new way of keeping milk fresh. He had been looking for a way to help the wine makers of France keep their wines from going sour, when he discovered that he could kill bacteria with heat. His process of heating milk to keep it from spoiling is called pasteurization. The discovery came none too soon because children were suffering from a painful kind of tuberculosis carried by cows. In countries that pasteurize their milk, the disease is gone, but where people drink raw milk, there is still the risk of getting this deadly disease.

Now we can dry milk, evaporate it, condense it, and of course, keep it in a refrigerator. No longer does the cream freeze at the top of milk bottles because the cream is all mixed in. We have learned how to homogenize it, which is a way of breaking down the fatty cream so that it no longer separates. We have skim milk, with no fat at all, and two-percent milk, with half the normal amount of fat. And of course we have chocolate milk, milk shakes, and ice cream.

To supply everyone with these modern milk products, we have to use modern methods. Herds of hundreds of dairy cows are led into clean milking parlors twice a day, where they are milked by machines more quickly than people can do it. The milk flows directly from the cow's udder through stainless steel pipes to cooling tanks. From there it goes into stainless steel tank trucks and then to dairies, where it will be pasteurized and then homogenized or skimmed or made into butter or ice cream.

Beef cattle are fattened in feeder lots before they are shipped to slaughterhouses, where their carcasses are cut into meat. Their hides are sent to tanneries to be made into leather, and their bones sent on to manufacturers who will use them to make fertilizer, glue, and dozens of other products. Nothing is wasted.

For the most part, milk and beef cows live comfortable lives, even in large herds. But veal calves are not so lucky. People prize veal because the meat is lean, white, and tender. In order to get that meat, veal producers buy day-old calves and keep them in tiny stalls where the animals can't move around very much. Moving would make their muscles strong and the meat less tender. The calves are fed a high-fat milk substitute, which fattens them quickly but keeps the meat white. By the time the calves are fifteen weeks old and weigh about three hundred pounds, they are ready for slaughter. Although only a few hundred thousand calves are used for veal each year, it seems an unnecessary and cruel way to treat any creature.

The contented, cud-chewing cow is more than a simple vending machine. It is one of the animals that changed the way people live.

6 Who Penned the Pig?

Priscilla loved to swim. One hot Texas afternoon, this small black and white pig was paddling in a cool lake with her owner's neighbors, eleven-year-old Anthony Burk and his mother. Suddenly Anthony hit a deep cold spot. He gulped a mouthful of water and went under. He surfaced but then choked and sank again. His mother raced toward him, but the pig got there first. Exhausted, and flailing out for anything to hang on to, Anthony grabbed Priscilla's harness. But the boy was four times bigger than the young pig, and his weight pulled Priscilla under, too. The little pig finally struggled to the surface and pulled Anthony to shore. Priscilla was the first pig to win a place in the Texas Pet Hall of Fame, and she was honored on Priscilla the Pig Day in Houston in August 1984.

If you ask people what they think of pigs, some will say, "Yuck, smelly." But others will tell you they're intelligent. Both are right. Pigs do get smelly when they root around in the mud.

Although real pigs may not be as clever as Miss Piggy, they can be taught to do anything dogs can do. Pig owners say their pets learn faster and are easier to housebreak than puppies, too.

For hundreds of years, pigs in France have rooted out underground mushrooms called truffles. Truffles are so delicious and so scarce today that people are willing to pay two hundred dollars a pound for them. A good truffle pig can smell the deeply buried mushrooms from twenty feet away. Most pigs provide ham, bacon, pork chops, and pigskin, of course. But they can also stand guard, sniff out land mines, pull carts, give real piggyback rides, or like Priscilla, swim to the rescue.

Pigs of one kind or another have been on earth for 36 million years, about ten times longer than humans. There are many kinds, such as bush pigs, wild boars, warthogs, peccaries, and giant forest pigs. All of them are stubborn, independent animals, and tough in battle. One swipe of a wild boar's sharp tusk can slice open almost any opponent. Their hollow tusks never stop growing. The lower tusks wear off as they work against upper teeth, but the top tusks curve around and around as the pig gets older. On the island of New Guinea in the Pacific Ocean, curved boar tusks were once used for money. The more curled the tusk, the more it was worth.

It was the wild boar that became the ancestor of today's domestic pigs. Wild boars are lean, long-legged, and covered with bristly hair. They have long snouts, short erect ears, and straight tails.

Scientists say that pigs were easy to domesticate because they

aren't specialized. They don't eat just one thing or need to live in one particular habitat. Like us, they are omnivores, which means they eat both plants and animals. They will even eat our leftovers. As long as they can find food, pigs stay in one place. That place can be thick forest, flat open plain, mountain, swamp, or village. As long as they are near water, pigs can live in almost any climate. Pigs have few sweat glands, so they must cool off in water or wallow in mud.

Like humans, pigs are *gregarious*. They like company. While they don't travel in herds, they do stick together, and that also made them easy to domesticate. Pigs were crop robbers. When people settled down to raise crops, pigs moved in to root through the gardens. Even now in parts of Southeast Asia, pigs are only half domesticated. They search for food in the forests during the day, but they return to the safety of villages at night.

The oldest known bones of domestic pigs were found in the Middle East and China. They were 8,500 years old. Egyptian farmers used hogs to "tred in the seeds" after a rain. A pig's pointed feet made just the right size hole in the soil and trampled the seeds to the right depth. After the grain was harvested, pigs helped with the threshing. They trotted over the grain, and their sharp hooves separated the husks from the kernels.

During the Middle Ages, peasants weren't allowed to use dogs to help them hunt in some of the forests. For more than four hundred years they used trained pigs instead. The pigs could hunt as well as any dog, and sometimes better. A hunting pig that belonged to Sir Henry Mildmay in the 1800s became famous for her skill. She was said to "find, point, and retrieve Game as well as the best Pointer." And "when called to go out Shooting, she would come home off the forest at full stretch."

Centuries before Captain Cook happened upon Hawaii, the islands had been settled by Polynesians. These courageous people had sailed thousands of miles across the Pacific Ocean in huge open sailing canoes that carried fifty people, as well as pigs, dogs, and chickens. They had come prepared to stay. They ate dogs — as people did in many countries — as often as pigs and chickens. But pigs were different. They were respected animals in old Hawaii. A man who owned pigs was not only rich, he was important in the community. But after the English sailors arrived, the Hawaiians were so eager to get iron nails that they would trade one of their valuable hogs for one nail.

In 1778, Captain Cook noted in his ship's log that he saw a lot of curly-tailed pigs running about the houses in Hawaii. He probably didn't know that the curly tail proves that those pigs had been domesticated for a long time. Any pig with long floppy ears, a stubby snout, a short curly tail, or not much hair came from domesticated grandparents.

In the Middle Ages, each town hired a swine herdsman to watch over all the pigs and make sure they didn't roam too far. It was an easy way to keep pigs because they foraged for themselves. But as forests were cut down to make room for more farms and towns, pigs had a harder time finding food. They roamed farther away, and that's when farmers began to keep their pigs in sties or pigpens.

Once each farmer kept his own pigs, the real domestication of pigs began. Pigs became what the farmer wanted. A pig could be bred for more meat but less fat, for example. The more than three hundred different breeds of domestic pigs that exist today are raised either for lard or for bacon, ham, and other cuts of pork. The black Berkshire pigs that are bred for their high quality meat came to America from England in 1823. Hereford pigs were developed in the United States in the early 1900s for their thick layer of fat that makes good lard. An all-white pig called the Chester White was bred in Chester, Pennsylvania, for its bacon.

Most pigs got bigger and bigger. An average adult pig weighs about eight hundred pounds. The record goes to a pig called Big Boy from North Carolina. He weighed 1,904 pounds, about the weight of a small car. On the other end of the scale is a dwarf pig called the S-1. It was bred to be used in laboratory research, because smaller animals are easier to handle.

Breeders of the S-1 were surprised at the little pig's popularity. People buy them as pets, even though the pigs weigh 225 pounds when they grow up.

Pigs came to the New World from all over the globe. When Columbus landed on the island of Haiti, he left eight pigs there. Years later, when other ships stopped at Haiti, sailors found that the descendants of these once-tame pigs had gone back to the wild. The feral pigs had become lean and rangy, with teeth like razors. Red Guinea hogs came on the slave ships from Africa. East Indian hogs, Russian hogs, English Berkshire hogs, and white hogs from the Netherlands and Sweden arrived in the colonies, and from all these came the pigs that would make up the American breeds.

A historian describing the plantations of Virginia and Maryland in the 1770s said, "The planter might love his horse, admire his cattle, but he respected his hogs." The hogs may have been respected, but they didn't get much care. They were turned loose in the forests to find their own food. All the farmer did was "harvest" his pigs each fall. Some farmers did bring their hogs into pens to fatten them on corn for a few weeks just before it was time to kill them because a ham from a corn-fed hog tastes good. Every part of the pig was used, right down to the intestines, which were cleaned and used as casings for sausage.

No more than a hundred years ago, most Americans lived on farms or in small, sprawling towns, where they could keep a cow, a few chickens, and a pig or two. Their animals were "ready to hand." No one thought it strange to see a herd of cattle driven through city streets or chickens in the backyard or pigs rooting around in garbage. In 1842, there were ten thousand pigs in New York City.

Most pig farming today is big business. Pigs are raised scientifically, with food measured out in just-right amounts, with just-right vitamins added. The goal is leaner meat, because people don't want fatty bacon and pork. Some of the sheds are air-conditioned. On the huge farms, there are no comfortable mud wallows, no loose barn boards where a pig can scratch an itchy back, and no more apples from a friendly visitor. Now one farmer can raise ten or twelve thousand pigs. In the United States, 75 million pigs are slaughtered each year, after they've been fed half of the nation's corn crop. Those pigs give us ham, pork chops, bacon, lard, pickled pigs' feet (which some people actually like to eat), and about five hundred other products.

Pigskin is good leather because it breathes. That means that the pores or bristle holes go right through. (Footballs are called pigskins, but now they are made from cowhide). A very thin layer of pigskin can be sterilized and specially treated to stick without any adhesive. It's used to cover painful burns while a patient's own skin grows back.

Pigs are used in medical research because their bodies work so much like ours. Insulin is a hormone made in the pancreas. It regulates the level of sugar in the blood. When a person's pancreas isn't making enough insulin, the result is a disease called diabetes. But it can be treated with insulin collected from the pancreases of pigs that have been slaughtered for meat. We also use dozens of pig-made chemicals to treat arthritis, leukemia, and other diseases.

While domestic pigs are being so useful, wild pigs are causing big problems. Early in the 1900s, wild boars were shipped from Europe to a game farm in North Carolina because hunters wanted the challenge of tracking and killing these feisty animals. By the 1920s, some wild boars had escaped from the game farm. They and their great-grandchildren have enjoyed life ever since in the Great Smoky Mountains. Nobody cared until the hogs moved into the national park, where they compete for food with black bears and other animals. Park rangers call the wild hogs Rototillers on legs because they plow up the soil and destroy plants.

California has the same problem. Wild pigs from Anadel State Park have been raiding golf courses and gardens. One reporter said, "To the pigs, the town was a well-stocked salad

bar." Some of the wild pigs are descendants of domesticated pigs the Spanish settlers brought with them in the 1760s. Others are true wild pigs, with short upright ears, long snouts, and long thick tails with tufts at the ends. These pigs came to California in 1925, when a group of hunters bought them from a breeder in North Carolina. According to the law, the pigs had to be fenced in, and they were. But some escaped. The wild pigs mixed and mated with the once-domestic feral pigs, and their numbers are growing. They are wrecking a lot of land and destroying a lot of plants. One biologist opened up a dead pig and found two thousand rare lily bulbs in its stomach.

At the Haleakala National Park on the island of Maui in Hawaii, rangers had to build a fence five feet high around the entire twenty-eight thousand acres to keep out feral goats and pigs. And so it goes. Pigs are stubborn, independent, intelligent, and tough. We domesticated them, but can we control them?

7

Who Cooped the Chicken?

More than a thousand years ago, a flock of geese saved a Roman army. The soldiers had fought hard all day, but they'd been forced back to a fort on a steep rocky hill. Guards were on duty, but they heard nothing in the still, dark night. Suddenly, a flock of geese cackled and honked. The racket woke the Roman soldiers. They grabbed their swords and raced to the fort wall just as the enemy soldiers were climbing it. The Romans won the battle, and since then, geese have stood guard at many battles and barnyards.

Domestic geese have been around for thousands of years. Besides guard duty, geese have provided eggs, meat, lard, warm down, and feathers. No one knows exactly when or where, but someone in Europe made friends with wild greylag geese. And these streamlined gray geese gradually changed into domestic white farm geese. Konrad Lorenz is the scientist who showed how easily people and geese might have come together. He became the parent of a baby greylag goose without meaning to.

Dr. Lorenz was watching a tiny gosling hatch out of its egg. Just as it stepped out of the shell, the tiny goose stared at Dr. Lorenz with one shiny dark eye. Like most birds, a goose uses one eye when it wants to see something clearly. Dr. Lorenz remembers that he said a few words, and the gosling answered in a soft, hissing whisper.

Then Dr. Lorenz tucked the gosling under the feathers of an old goose. He was certain the young one would think it was nestling under its mother's wing. But he was wrong. "Instead of being comforted," Dr. Lorenz said, "as any sensible goose child should have been, mine came out from the warm feathers, and 'weeping' loudly, ran away from her, calling 'pfeep, pfeep, pfeep.' This is approximately the sound of the piping of 'being left alone' of the greylag gosling.

"The rest of my day passed just as it passes for a goose mother," Dr. Lorenz said. That first night, the gosling slept under a heating pad in a tiny basket next to Dr. Lorenz's bed. Every hour, the gosling peeped the *weeweewee* call, which was its way of saying, "Here I am. Where are you?" And Dr. Lorenz learned to answer in greylag language, *gangangang*.

For the rest of its life, that goose followed Dr. Lorenz everywhere. Dr. Lorenz had been imprinted on the gosling in those first moments after hatching, when he answered its stare. Usually the first thing a hatchling sees is its mother. But whoever "speaks" to it first is imprinted on the gosling's brain as clearly

as a message that says, "This is your mother. Stick with her."

Imagine how that imprinting must have happened again and again to many people in many places. And once geese stayed close to people, they began to change. Well-fed geese are too bulky to fly, but that made them easier to keep in one place. So the greylag lost its streamlined looks and became fatter.

Some geese became so fat that they made farmers rich. In France, cooks make a food called pâté de foie gras. It's mashed up goose liver, with added seasonings. A goose's liver isn't very big. To make the livers larger, farmers force-feed the geese with extra corn two or three times a day.

One of the best gifts from geese is their soft layer of down. These are the fluffy feathers that lie under the waterproof top feathers like insulated underwear. The first person who stuffed goose down between two pieces of cloth made the warmest and softest covering ever invented. There are all kinds of man-made linings, but down is still the best.

Eider ducks are famous for their down. They live on rocky shores in the Arctic, where they need a lot of down feathers to line their nests and cover their eggs. An eiderdown quilt is lighter than feathers, and more expensive than any other because it's not easy to collect the down. Collectors disturbed so many eggs in eider duck nests in Iceland and Norway that now the nesting colonies have been fenced in. Strict rules set a limit on the amount of down a person can take.

Muscovy ducks were domesticated in South America, and mallard ducks in China about two thousand years ago. The

American Poultry Association says there are twelve kinds of domestic ducks. Some were bred for meat, some for eggs, and some just because they're nice to look at in garden ponds.

Red jungle fowl are the great-grandparents of all chickens. Four thousand years ago in the Middle East, children probably were sent to search for eggs in the hidden nests of red jungle fowl hens. The hens are bland brown shades that blend with their background. But the rooster has shiny, reddish brown feathers that curve into a long plumy tail. His head is topped off by a bright red comb. Red jungle fowl still live in the jungles of Asia, but they have many look-alike relatives in barnyards all over the world.

Two things made it easy to tame the red jungle fowl. First, the hens stay in a rooster's territory, where they roost in low tree branches early in the evening. Second, they are *precocial* (pre-KO-shul). A precocial bird is one that can leave the nest right after it's hatched. It can find its own food, but it is imprinted on its mother and stays close to her for protection.

It would have been easy to lure jungle fowl close to a village by scattering grain. People may have shooed the birds into pens to keep them safe from animals that hunt in the dark. As years went by, the jungle fowl changed, but not much. They didn't have to work so hard to find food or to protect themselves from predators, so they grew plump. And their wing muscles weakened because they didn't fly far. But they behaved much the same as their wild cousins.

Red jungle fowl

Domestic

When two roosters fight for a territory, they crouch low and hold their wings high to protect their heads. They pounce and attack each other with blows from their strong beaks. Usually they quit before one gets killed. But in some parts of the world, people bred the fiercest roosters and trained them to fight to the death. They strapped sharp curved blades on the roosters' legs like spurs, so they'd slash one another. Rooster fights are cruel. They've been outlawed in most countries, but not everywhere.

Like dogs and cats, chickens moved around the world in overland caravans as well as by sea. The Polynesians had chickens aboard when they made the long voyage across the Pacific Ocean to Hawaii in large sailing canoes. Spanish explorers took chickens to North and South America five hundred years ago.

But turkeys were here all the time. Wild turkeys are native American birds, but they were *not* served at the first Thanksgiving dinner. That menu included wild plums, wild rice, venison, duck, geese, eels and other fish, vegetables, and puddings. The fat, white domestic turkeys we eat for holiday meals had their start in Mexico. The southern version of the wild turkey is more brightly colored, with fancy feathers of shimmering blue, green, bronze, and gold. These were the birds that were domesticated.

Domestic turkeys are smaller than the wild ones. Wild tom turkeys sometimes weigh fifty pounds, but they can fly short distances. Domestic turkeys can't fly because they are bred for more breast meat. They're too top-heavy to take off. But they

Wild

Domestic

are safe behind fences, where they don't have to watch for predators. Their brains are smaller than those of their wild cousins, and they probably wouldn't survive long in the forest.

In the ruins of ancient Rome many thousands of years old, someone found instructions for poultry keeping: Hens should be fattened, and the chicken house should be near the kitchen so smoke from the cooking fire would blow among the chickens and kill their lice.

Domestic chickens no longer live by the rules of wild jungle fowl. And the only old Roman rule we follow for keeping them is the part about fattening the hens. Few domestic chickens or turkeys scratch the ground for juicy bugs and worms or take dust baths to get rid of mites and lice. Few live in small flocks ruled by one rooster. They no longer roost early in the evening and get up at dawn to the rooster's crow.

Poultry farming has become more factory than farm, and the birds more product than animal. Modern chickens and turkeys live in air-conditioned coops under artificial light. Their food is delivered on moving belts. Their eggs are collected by other moving belts. One New York state egg farm raises 570,000 chickens. This farm won an award as a "Hen Haven" by a national poultry committee. It was judged for "cleanliness, well-maintained driveways and buildings, and the health of its livestock." The hen houses are controlled by computers. They are programmed to switch ventilation fans on or off, to adjust the temperature and lights, and to send an alarm if anything

goes wrong. Only six people are allowed in the hen houses of
that farm because they don't want to expose the chickens to
disease. Chickens can catch a deadly bronchitis that can wipe
out a whole flock.

On one midwestern farm, twenty-seven thousand chickens
are raised in a shed thirty feet wide and almost as long as two
football fields. The farmer has three other sheds just like it. To
keep the birds active and eating, the farmer keeps the lights on
twenty-three hours a day. The one hour of darkness is not to
give the chickens a rest but to get them used to the dark so
they won't panic if the power goes out. In such a henhouse, it

can be forever spring. Long stretches of light trigger the birds' egg-laying systems, just as the longer days of spring will do after the short days of winter.

On small farms it once took sixteen weeks to raise a hen that weighed two pounds. Now, chickens called broilers are ready for market in seven or eight weeks, when they weigh four pounds. In the 1920s the average hen laid 120 eggs a year. Now an average hen lays 250 eggs.

Breeders are always looking for ways to develop new kinds of "superchickens." For example, a "minihen" that is about two-thirds the size of an ordinary hen allows egg producers to keep more birds in one cage. Vitamin D added to chicken feed takes the place of sunlight. Antibiotics are added to food to keep the chickens from getting sick. Other chemicals add color and flavor to the meat and eggs.

Some poultry farms only hatch eggs and sell baby chicks. Others only produce and sell eggs, and others sell only the grown chickens. About 250 million hens lay the eggs used in this country, and more than three billion chickens are raised on the farm-factories that specialize in meat chickens.

Domestication has certainly changed the chicken!

8

Ship of the Desert

On May 14, 1856, thirty-four camels plodded down the gangplank of the ship that had carried them from Arabia to Texas. Forty-four more camels arrived nine months later. Together, these were the U.S. Army's first and last camel herd. For ten years they lived at Camp Verde near San Antonio. When the army was ordered to survey a new wagon road from Fort Defiance, New Mexico, to the Colorado River on the California border, twenty-five camels led the expedition. The camels worked well in the rugged country. They even swam across a river that had drowned ten mules and two horses. But their unit was dismissed anyway, and they were sold for thirty-one dollars each. The problem was the people, not the camels. The soldiers hadn't learned the art of camel handling.

Australia had a far different experience with camels. When the first breeding herd of twenty-four camels arrived in Australia in 1860, three camel trainers came with them. By 1925, there were thirteen thousand camels, which were used to draw carts, wagons, buggies, and farm equipment. It looked as though camels were going to be important animals in the Australian outback. And they were for about forty years. Then their job was taken over by railroads, trucks on superhighways, and cargo airlines. By 1966, only five hundred domestic camels were left. Most of the others had gone back to the wild. The feral camels became such a nuisance that they were called vermin or pests. There was a bounty on their heads, which meant that the government paid a reward to each hunter who proved he had killed a camel.

A camel is an all-purpose animal. It can be milked, ridden, or harnessed to a plow. It can carry twice as much baggage as a pair of oxen. Its meat can be eaten, its wool made into fine camel-hair coats, and its hide can be turned into good leather. Even its dried manure can be used for fuel. A camel can go ten days without water and can walk on soft ground where a truck would get stuck. Without the camel, people could not have crossed deserts or built settlements in dry lands.

If camels are so useful, why aren't they as common as cows or horses? Why were they domesticated so long after goats and sheep?

For one thing, the camel isn't an easy animal to get close to. It is ornery, stubborn, and smelly. It kicks hard enough to kill, and it spits a disgusting wad of goop. A camel is called the ship of the desert because it sails across the sand on soft, padded feet, swaying like a ship at sea. The camel has a rolling gait

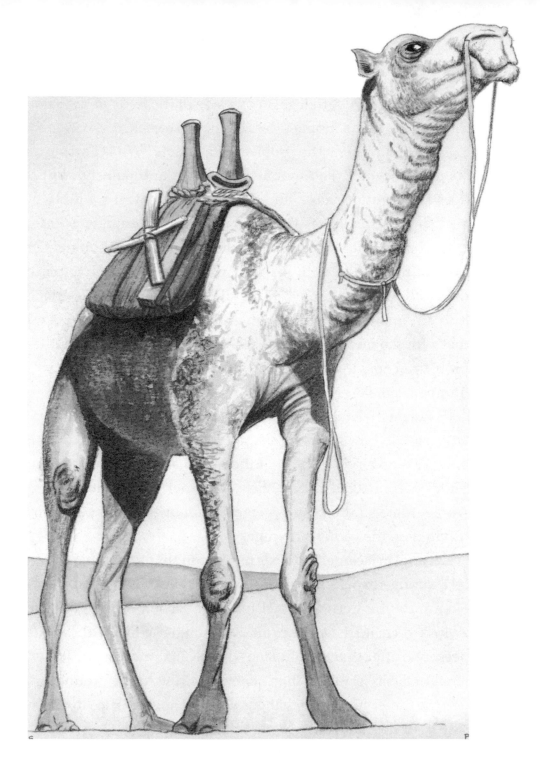

because it moves both legs on one side of the body at the same time when it runs. Some riders even get seasick.

And then there is the problem of a saddle. What do you do about the hump? The mound is not soft and squishy, but it does bend out of shape under a heavy weight. It's a lump of fat that gets smaller as the fat is used up for energy. A rider either has to put weight directly over the camel's shoulders in front of the hump, with his feet on the camel's neck, or place the saddle over the camel's rear end behind the hump, or attach it to a framework that rests on either side of the hump. And that's for the one-humped camel, called the dromedary. Other problems come up when a rider climbs on the Bactrian or two-humped camel.

In northern Arabia, the best saddle was devised with two large saddle bows, arches shaped like upside-down *v*'s. Each bow rests on a pad in front of the hump and on a pad behind. They are connected by two sticks. Another pad is put over this whole frame so the rider's weight is not on the hump but distributed on the camel's rib cage.

Getting on a camel saddle is hard enough, but getting off can be a strange experience, too. One rider described what it was like, once you get the camel to kneel: "Then down goes the awkward creature by the front, and you hang forward over its neck; and after that the hind legs double up, and you are jerked straight again, and can then slide gracefully to the ground unless the camel suddenly changes its mind and gets up, in which case your descent is more spectacular."

An ancient picture shows two riders on a camel, one facing back and the other front. Either this unknown Arabian tribe didn't have enough camels, or one man handled the camel while the other threw spears or shot arrows. Camels were often used in warfare. They are taller than horses, which gives the rider an advantage because he can see farther, and they can go through drifting sand that would stop a horse. The present-day Jordanian Desert Corps takes pride in its camels, which can patrol where even a four-wheel-drive vehicle is useless.

Despite any inconvenience to a rider, a camel is perfect for the desert. Its thick coat is insulation against the desert's hot days and cold nights. Its nostrils close against blowing sand, and its eyes are protected by overhanging lids and long, thick lashes. A camel can fill up on thirty gallons of water in ten minutes and doesn't lose it in sweat. A camel's body temperature can safely rise eleven degrees! If we didn't cool off our bodies by sweating, and if our body temperature went up even four or five degrees, we'd be in serious trouble.

The camel came a long, roundabout way to domestication. Millions of years ago, the first camels lived in North America. They were not much bigger than rabbits. During the first Ice Age, when great glaciers moved over the continent, some of these ancient camel ancestors migrated toward South America. Others migrated across the land bridge that connected Asia and North America, and those left behind became extinct. Eventually, in the slow way of evolution, those ancient camel-creatures changed into the long-legged camels of today.

Ancient camel ancestors:

Alticamelus

Procamelus

Scientists say that all the one-humped camels alive today are either domesticated or feral — the descendants of once-domesticated camels. Even after thousands of years of domestication, the dromedary hasn't changed very much, although there are several breeds. One is the long-legged mehari, or riding camel. Others are bred for use as pack animals, and others to supply milk and wool.

The one-humped camel did not start out in Egypt, where tourists now ride them past the great pyramids. Egyptians didn't even have a word for camel when dromedaries went to work in Arabia about four thousand years before the birth of Christ. As long as Middle Eastern countries had rich pasturelands, people didn't need camels. But gradually, the climate changed, and long years of drought turned vast areas to desert. Then camels became so important that in some places they replaced carts and wagons. A wagon drawn by oxen needs a driver for every two animals, but one person can handle a string of six camels. Wagons get stuck in sand, but camels keep going longer, over rougher ground, carrying twice the weight. It's no wonder that camels became the "ships" that nomads could depend upon to move them across the desert from one oasis to the next.

The two-humped Bactrian camel has a different story. These hardy camels with their longer, thicker hair are adapted to the colder weather of Central Asia and northern China. For thousands of years they have been hitched to plows and wagons, but they are most famous for their long treks across mountains and plains. Without the camel caravans, there would have been no way for traders of incense, silk, and spices to travel overland from the Orient to Europe.

Four cousins of the camel live in the mountains of South America. They are called llamoids — llamas, alpacas, vicuñas, and guanacos. The guanaco developed from the prehistoric rabbit-size camel that migrated south millions of years ago. All the llamoids have short bodies, long legs, long necks, small heads, and pointed ears. The first Europeans to see them in South America called them Indian sheep. Instead of the wide flat feet that carry camels over sand, the guanaco cousins developed smaller feet that give them sure footing on the steep mountain trails of the Andes Mountains. None of the llamoids has a hump, but they all spit like camels. And they are all known for their stubbornness. A llama, for example, can carry about 130 pounds on its back, and it lets everyone know when a load is too heavy. It spits, hisses, kicks, or simply lies down until the load is lightened.

From the wild guanaco, the Inca Indians created the domesticated llama, alpaca, and vicuña thousands of years ago. No one knows which came first, but each had a different purpose. The llama, which has an easy scientific name to remember, *Llama glama*, was and still is an all-purpose animal. It provides transportation, meat, wool, hides, and dried dung for fuel. Every two years the female llamas are sheared, and each one yields seven or eight pounds of wool. The males used as pack animals are not sheared because their thick fleece makes a natural cushion under the loads piled on their backs.

A thousand years ago, in the days of the great ancient Inca civilization, llamas were also used in religious ceremonies. On the first day of each month, one hundred pure white llamas were sacrificed to keep the sun gods happy. The meat was thrown into fires, and the bones were ground up into fine powder for medicine and magic. To use that many white llamas, the Inca farmers must have had to breed and raise them.

Alpacas are shaggier than llamas, with long bangs that hang over their eyes like sheepdogs' bangs. They were bred for their wool, which is as soft as goose down. People pay high prices to buy coats and scarves made from alpaca. In the Inca com-

Llamas

Vicuna

Guanaco

Alpaca

munities, domestic herds of llamas and alpacas were owned by the state and guarded by shepherd boys between the ages of nine and sixteen. After the wool was sheared, it was given to the married women in the community, who spun it into yarn. The yarn was then passed on to other women who wove it into cloth.

Scientists are still arguing over the vicuña, which is the smallest of the llamoids and has the softest, most lustrous hair. Some say it is a wild animal. Others say it, too, was domesticated from the guanaco but was allowed to roam wild on purpose. The herds were rounded up each year for shearing and let go again. The few ounces of wool gathered from each animal was used only to make exquisite robes for the imperial Inca rulers, who were believed to be gods. It would have been one way to make sure there was always a big difference between clothes for royalty and ordinary people.

Llamas and their cousins carry their heads high, with the same haughty look of the camel. But they cannot go three days without food or water. Perhaps they learned from the camel's sad beginning, which Rudyard Kipling imagined in another of the *Just So Stories*.

At the beginning of the world, Camel was so haughty that he refused to carry or plow or do any work for three days. Horse and Dog and Ox complained to the Djinn (magician) in charge of All Deserts. But all Camel would say is, "Humph!" After the Djinn warned Camel that he might say that once too often, Camel said it again. Djinn put the "humph" on Camel's back. "And from that day to this, the Camel always wears a humph (we call it a 'hump' now, not to hurt his feelings); but he has never yet caught up with the three days that he missed at the beginning of the world, and he has never yet learned how to behave."

9

Silk and Honey

Two thousand years ago, silk was worth its weight in gold. And no wonder. It takes a thousand *miles* of silk thread to make one pound of raw silk. How did anyone ever figure out how to make beautiful cloth from an insect's cocoon?

The silkworm is so domesticated that it can no longer live without help. In fact, the silkworm moth can't even fly anymore. All caterpillars produce silken threads that harden in the air as they are spun from the silk glands in the caterpillars' mouths. They use the thread to build cocoons. But the domestic silkworm spins a silk like no other. Silk has been called the cloth of kings. It is so smooth that dirt doesn't cling to it and so elastic that cloth woven from it does not lose its shape easily. It is twice as strong as an iron wire the same size.

A Chinese legend thousands of years old tells of the empress Si Ling-Shi, who was having tea under a mulberry bush in the palace garden. She watched a fat white worm on a branch above

her as it moved its head back and forth, back and forth. From its mouth, the worm spun a shiny strand of golden thread, until it had wrapped itself inside a cocoon. It is said that the empress dropped the cocoon into her warm tea, perhaps by accident. When the cocoon was warm, the threads loosened, and the empress was able to unwind the silken thread. *Shi* has been the Chinese word for silk since then. Only women of the royal family fed the worms, unwound the silk, and wove it into cloth. For two thousand years, the Chinese people guarded the secret of the silkworm. Anyone caught stealing either a silkworm or its eggs was sentenced to death. Then, in the year 2630 B.C., Emperor Huang-ti ordered his wife to show the common people how to raise silkworms, and he opened the silkworm-raising season each year with great ceremony.

The silkworm of China is a large white moth, with the scientific name *Bombyx mori*. Its lovely wings are traced with black lines. Each female moth lays one batch of two hundred to five hundred eggs, which are put into cold storage. When the eggs hatch into tiny worms no thicker than a hair, they begin to eat mulberry leaves, and only mulberry leaves. Each day each worm eats its weight in leaves. For five weeks the rooms are filled with the sound of crunching. When the worm is about three inches long and as thick as a man's little finger, it begins to spin its silk cocoon. Around and around in a figure eight, it winds silk for three days. Now the finished cocoons are sent to factories where the silk is unwound by machines. Two or three thousand feet of silk thread can be taken from one cocoon. But for many centuries, women warmed the cocoons and unwound each one by hand. Their method was carefully guarded. Chinese silk cloth was sold to other countries, but only the finished cloth and never the thread or the worms.

But gradually the secret of silk crept out. One Chinese princess who was about to marry a prince from another country didn't want to give up her silk making, so she hid some moth eggs in her thick hair and took them with her. The silk industry spread to Korea, Japan, and southern Asia. In the year 552, a Persian emperor sent some priests to China with orders to bring back silkworms. The few hardy worms that survived the trip hidden in hollow bamboo canes were enough to start the silk industry in Europe.

Silkworms are the only truly domesticated insects. Honeybees work for us, but they are free to pick up and leave when they want to. For good reason the people who work with bees are called keepers, not owners.

For thousands of years, honey was the only sweetener for food. The hunters and gatherers of the Stone Age must have watched bears break into beehives in hollow trees and dig out pawfuls of sticky honey. Then people learned to do it, too. And maybe by accident, after a forest fire, they discovered that smoke made the bees groggy — and safer to be around. After that, people probably used torches to smoke out the bees whenever they wanted fresh honey.

In Africa the honey guide bird loves to eat beeswax and grubs, but the bird isn't strong enough to break into bee nests inside tree trunks. So it has formed a partnership with the honey badger, a tough little animal that loves honey. The badger is built close to the ground, with skin so thick that a bee can't sting through it. When the badger sees the honey guide bird fluttering and screeching around a tree, it goes into action. One whiff of honey, and the badger scurries to the tree and rips out the hive with its long claws. People in Africa who love honey learned long ago to follow the screeching bird and beat the badger to the honey.

When a honeybee flies from flower to flower, it's collecting two things — pollen and nectar. The pollen from a flower contains the sperm. It has to get to the female part of a flower so the plant can produce seeds. The bee collects pollen in the pollen baskets on its legs. When the bee stops at the next flower

of the same kind, some pollen is left behind to fertilize that flower. Without honeybees, farmers would be in big trouble. They'd have no way of getting a new crop of apples, pears, clover, or most any plant. The rest of the pollen in the bee's leg baskets gets back to the hive, where it is stored as bee bread that will feed the growing young bees called grubs.

But it is the sweet nectar from flowers that turns into honey. When a bee sips the thin, watery liquid from a blossom, the nectar goes into a "honey bag" pouch inside the bee's body. There it is digested into two kinds of sugar, levulose and dextrose. Once the bee has deposited the sugars in the cells of the hive, most of the water evaporates and the sugars become thicker. That's honey.

The flavor of the honey depends on the kind of flower it comes from. Alfalfa and clover are the most common kinds of honey. White honey is made from orange blossoms or white sage. Buckwheat honey is rich and dark. In the fall, bees also make dark honey from goldenrod.

Beekeeping is a matter of knowing how bees live and staying a step ahead of their needs. Good beekeepers have to know that the queen bee controls the hive and lays all the eggs. She is the mother of the whole colony. Without her, the other bees have no purpose. The worker bees feed her, take care of the eggs, collect nectar and pollen, and make wax and honey. They are the furnace in winter and the air conditioner in summer. With wings beating like little fans, the worker bees can heat up or cool off the hive. Worker bees also stand guard at the en-

trance to the hive and turn away all intruders, including bees from other hives.

The male bees are called drones, and they have only one important job. They fertilize the millions of eggs produced by the queen bee. Bees, of course, come from eggs laid by the queen. There is no king in the hive. She can lay as many as two thousand eggs in a day, and in her four or five years of life, that adds up to about two million eggs. Each egg is laid in a cell made of wax, which is also made by the worker bees. Other layers of these six-sided cells are used to store honey, which is their food for the winter.

When a worker bee is about ten days old, she can make wax from glands on the underside of her abdomen. As bits of scaly wax come out, she chews and molds them into place to build and repair the cells. When she's twenty days old, she may do guard duty at the door to make sure no foreign bees get into the hive. It is only the older workers that fly out to bring back pollen, nectar, water, and propolis, which is also called bee glue. Bees collect the sticky propolis from buds on trees and use it to seal up cracks and change the size of the hive.

Even though bees have been around for millions of years, we haven't cracked all their codes. But we certainly know more of their secrets than people did when they began to keep bees. One ancient "recipe" for bees says that honeybees come from oxen. All you have to do is put a dead ox in a room, sprinkle it with an herb called thyme, then seal the room. After three weeks, open the room for a short time, then seal it again. When the door is opened after eleven more days, swarms of bees will be waiting to get out. The "king" of the bees in this swarm was said to come from the brain of the ox. The recipe doesn't say how to get rid of the awful smell and mess in the room.

Lorenzo Langstroth, an American beekeeper, discovered that bees will always leave a space one-fourth to three-eighths of an inch between the combs. A comb is a section of thousands of wax cells. Worker bees keep building cells until there is no room for more, and they fill those cells with honey. The one-fourth inch space between that comb and the edge of the bee-keeper's box is filled in with bee glue and capped over with beeswax. Mr. Langstroth's discovery was important to bee-keepers because they know that if they add layers on top of their bee boxes, the bees will keep building cells and filling them with honey. Beekeepers take only the extra honey the bees don't need for food.

We use beeswax the way people did long ago — for candles, for molding artificial fruits and flowers, for cosmetics and ointments. But we also use it to make furniture polish, waxed paper, and some kinds of printing ink — a lot of products from a tiny animal.

In the Stone Age, an artist living in the land we now call Spain painted a picture on a cave wall of a person collecting honey from wild honeybees. Much later, but still some 4,500 years ago, Egyptians left records on temple walls about bee-keeping. Today's beekeepers may have better equipment and more protection with cover-up bee suits, but the bees they are tending are no different from those the Stone Age artist painted. Some specialists have tried to domesticate bees by breeding new queens, but so far it hasn't made much difference. The bees still live as they have for millions of years: free, but on loan to humans.

10 All Creatures Small

A fat white bunny in a pet shop, a guinea pig in a cage at school, a pigeon that takes popcorn from your hand, or a tiny goldfish carried home from the fair in a plastic bag — were they ever wild? They don't seem so, but of course they were.

Rabbits reproduce fast. By the time a female wild rabbit is four months old, she is ready to have her first litter. In thirty days she can produce eight or nine babies, and she can have six litters during the spring and summer of one year. If all the babies from just *one pair* of rabbits lived to have babies, there would be more than 33 million rabbits in three years! Of course they don't all live. Nine out of ten of them are eaten by hunters: hawks, wolves, owls, snakes, coyotes, cougars, bobcats, and people.

Where there are no predators to eat them, rabbits can take over the land. In 1859, twenty-four rabbits arrived in Australia

on the ship *Lightning*. They were set free on a ranch, where they began to reproduce at lightning speed. They mowed down all the grass and shrubs meant for sheep. Five rabbits ate as much as one sheep! In three years, millions of rabbits turned thousands of square miles of pasture into dust. Farmers tried to fight back by selling rabbit meat and fur and stringing thousands of miles of fences that were supposed to be rabbit-proof, but the rabbits got through. And the rabbits didn't stop their march across Australia until the 1950s, when a disease killed most of them.

But just the opposite happened in 1951, when twenty thousand rabbits were let loose in New Jersey for hunters. It cost the state twenty-seven thousand dollars to raise and take the rabbits out to the fields, but by the time hunting season opened, only 1,600 rabbits were left. Other predators had gotten to them first.

In almost every country, rabbits have provided food and clothing since people lived in caves. The ancient rabbits were not much different from wild rabbits of today. They, too, were easy to trap and good to eat, and their fur was soft and warm. American Plains Indians once had rabbit drives in the autumn. Lined up shoulder to shoulder, the Indians marched through fields, driving the rabbits ahead of them into traps. In this way, they got enough meat to dry for the winter and skins to make warm clothing.

The ancient Romans kept wild rabbits in walled gardens, where they could catch a few when they needed meat. They especially liked the tender meat from laurices, which was the name for newborn rabbits. During the Middle Ages, in the 1400s and 1500s, laurices provided a good reason to domesticate rabbits. On certain days of celebration, the Catholic church forbade people to eat red meat but allowed them to eat the white meat of fish and newborn rabbits. That's when monks in French monasteries began to breed rabbits for food.

Now farmers breed dozens of different kinds of domestic rabbits. Dwarf rabbits raised for pets weigh only three pounds, but the giant varieties raised for meat weigh as much as twenty pounds. They come in coats of white, black, chocolate, blue-gray, gold, and mixed patterns. White Angora rabbits are sheared four times a year, and their fine, silky fur is spun into fluffy yarn.

Domestic rabbits have bigger litters than their wild cousins, and they can have them in any season. But a domestic rabbit wouldn't last long if it were turned loose to live in the wild again. Domestication has left rabbits with smaller brains and smaller hearts. They don't have the keen senses of smell, sight, or hearing that help wild rabbits stay alive. On the other hand, domestic rabbits don't need those traits, especially as pets. People enjoy rabbits because they are affectionate, and they don't bark or scratch furniture. It's also easy to teach them to use a litter box.

As farm animals, rabbits are cheap to raise, and they don't take up much space. They don't eat expensive grain, and their meat has very little fat. If our planet ever gets so crowded with people that there's no more room for big beef cattle to graze, we may all be eating farm-raised rabbits.

We are already eating farm-raised fish. The Chinese people were the first to select and breed fish. A Chinese legend a thousand years old tells of a terrible drought that lasted one hundred days. Emperor Ping pleaded with the gods to send rain. His prayers were answered. The gods sent rain, and with it came carp, the "heavenly miracles." From that time on, these golden fish were cared for by monks in holy temples, and anyone who caught or ate these fish was in for terrible punishment.

Chinese carp are the ancestors of goldfish. The fish swam in garden ponds, so the monks bred varieties that would look beautiful when seen from above. Over the years, the fish changed in size, color, and shape. Some species developed long, graceful tails and shimmering transparent scales. They became more colorful — some white, black, deep gold, or red,

and some with calico patterns of blue spots. They were given such names as lionhead, bubble-eye, pearl scale, pompom, celestial, and butterfly. Most of these fancy mutations could not survive in the wild. The celestial, for example, with bugged-out eyes that always look toward heaven, couldn't compete with other fish in foraging for food on the bottom of a pond. And the lionhead, with its swollen bumpy head that looks like a raspberry, can't even get its own food at all. It must be fed by hand.

By the 1500s, Japanese fish breeders had filled their garden ponds with other varieties of golden carp called koi. For centuries, the Chinese and Japanese breeders kept their methods secret. Raising goldfish is a risky business. "Anything can happen and usually does," says one breeder. "For every hundred eggs laid, there may be only six or eight saleable offspring." Diseases and parasites can kill young fish or leave them too unhealthy to sell.

There is no average size to a goldfish. Their size depends on their environment. A goldfish raised in a small tank might be three inches long, but a fish from that same batch of eggs raised in a large outdoor pool could grow to ten inches. Their size also depends on their food supply and health.

The first goldfish arrived in England in 1691. People in the United States didn't see goldfish until P. T. Barnum displayed them at his circus in 1850. By 1865, New York City pet stores were selling goldfish by the thousands. Every year, more than 60 million goldfish are sold in this country, making them a bigger business than dogs or cats.

The plain brown cousin of the fancy goldfish is the common carp, which can live in almost any kind of water. Carp thrive in salty, brackish or fresh water. They are the scavengers that clean up the bottoms of lakes, ponds, and rivers. Carp are easy to catch and easy to raise in small ponds. In some parts of the southern United States, huge fish farms are raising channel carp by the hundreds of thousands. Farming fish for food has become a huge industry worth millions of dollars.

Fish and potatoes go together, especially on Idaho farms, where farmers are raising tilapia fish. The tilapia is a mild-flavored fish usually found in the Sea of Galilee and in lakes of Africa and South America. It's a plain gray or black, big-mouthed fish that grows to about fifteen inches long. The two kinds of farms are good partners, because the tilapia fish eat the leftovers from the potato crops.

In Norway, fish breeders are developing dwarf halibut fish.

In the open ocean, a halibut might weigh four hundred pounds by the time it's forty years old. The new breed will taste just the same, but it will be full grown in only three or four years, when it will weigh fifteen pounds. On Cape Cod, fish farmers are cultivating scallops, and in Japan, farmers raise octopus, squid, and oysters.

The ancient Romans knew that a young oyster was a tiny wormlike larva that swam around looking for a place to attach itself. So they put twigs in the water and waited for the oyster larvae to latch on and grow. Then all they had to do was haul the twigs out of the water to gather the oysters. In France and many other countries, oyster farmers use the same idea but with better equipment than twigs.

Oysters create pearls, which are made into beautiful jewelry. If a grain of sand or bit of coral gets inside an oyster's shell, it irritates the soft animal, like cracker crumbs in bed. The oyster can't scratch it or remove it, but it can cover the annoying spot with a smooth white substance called mother-of-pearl, the same material the oyster makes to line the inside of its shell. The longer the pearl is in the oyster's shell, the bigger it gets.

Pearls are expensive because a diver has to bring up oysters from deep in the ocean. It's a dangerous job, and a lot of it is guesswork. How can anyone know which oyster has a pearl? In the 1200s, the Chinese figured out a way to force oysters to make pearls. They made the first cultured pearls by opening freshwater mussel shells and inserting a tiny pellet of bone or wood inside. Then they'd close the mussel and put it back in its bed for three years. These pearls were beautiful, but they were blister pearls. One side of a blister pearl is flat, and two halves had to be put together in order to get one round bead.

In 1892, a Japanese pearl farmer, Kokichi Mikimoto, made the first whole cultured pearls. He inserted tiny beads of mother-of-pearl into saltwater pearl oysters with great success. Now there are more than two thousand cultured pearl farms in Japan. There are also farms in Australia and off the coast of California, and some of the finest cultured pearls come from the Persian Gulf.

Pigeons have been on the menu since almost the beginning of human life on earth. Today's pigeons are the descendants of the rock doves that roosted on rocky cliffs. In Egypt they nested on the ledges of pyramids. Rock doves were easy to trap. All a person had to do was toss a bit of grain on the ground and throw a net over the birds that gathered. In ancient Rome and Greece, where doves became a symbol of love and purity, the birds were often sacrificed to gods. But many more were eaten, especially the tender young pigeons, which are called squab.

A Bible story says that after forty days and forty nights of rain, Noah sent a white dove out from the ark to look for land. When the dove returned to the ark with an olive branch in its beak, Noah knew the flood was over. Doves or pigeons have been used to send messages since the earliest recorded times. A sultan of Baghdad had a pigeon postal system 3,100 years ago for his personal use. It wasn't a regular mail route for everyone.

Carrier pigeons stayed in business even after the telegraph was invented because telegraph equipment could break down. In war, armies depended on pigeons to carry messages when no human could get through enemy lines. A thousand miles is considered a long flight for a pigeon. But one United States Army Signal Corps pigeon flew 2,300 miles, a record for the longest wartime flight.

A built-in urge or instinct makes a homing pigeon head for its own loft. When birds are being trained for races, they are taken a short distance from their home loft and released. Gradually the birds learn to fly longer and longer distances. For an official race, each pigeon wears a tiny identification band around its leg. The birds are put into small carrying boxes and taken to the starting place. When all the birds are released at once, they rise and circle together in a great graceful swirl. In a moment they get their bearings and head for home. They may

Pigeon

Rock dove

have to fly through dangerous storms or hawk attacks, but they keep going until they get home.

If the pigeon circles over its loft or sits on the roof, it can't be counted home. Each bird has been trained to enter the loft through a small trap door. The race isn't over for a bird until the owner takes off the bird's leg band and drops it into a device that marks the time. The pigeon with the shortest time wins the race.

More than 250 different breeds of domestic pigeons provide meat, carry messages, race for sport, or show off fancy foot feathers and spreading fantails in competition. But the pigeons that roost on window ledges of skyscrapers, strut along city streets, and peck popcorn in the park are feral. They are the ancestors of pigeons that were once domesticated.

"The school is trying an experiment to teach math in a new way. You'll be the guinea pigs." If a teacher says that to a class, students know they are going to be the first group to try the new method. So many guinea pigs have been used in laboratories that their name has come to mean anything or anyone being used for an experiment.

Long before Spanish explorers arrived in South America, guinea pigs had been domesticated by the Inca Indians. One explorer in the 1800s wrote in his journal that guinea pigs "ran over and around the bodies of Indians sleeping all night long" in their huts. Guinea pigs still run loose in the houses of Indians who live in the Andes Mountains. But those guinea pigs aren't pets. They are being raised for food.

The ancestor of the domestic guinea pig is the wild cavy, which still lives in South America. It's a small brown rodent with a thick body, large head, short ears, and short legs. Domestic guinea pigs are rounder and thicker. The ones raised for pets come in different colors and hairstyles. There's a long-haired Angora that looks like a fuzzy mop, a blond with smooth fur, and a three-tone model in wide stripes of white, brown, and black, for example.

No one knows exactly where the wild cavy got the name guinea pig. Sixty-two years after Columbus discovered America, guinea pigs arrived in Europe on ships from South America. But on the way home, the ships stopped in Africa to pick up slaves. Part of Africa was called Guinea. That may have been the connection. Others say that guinea pigs look like baby

Wild cavy

African bush pigs called Guinea hogs. It probably doesn't matter where the name came from as long as we remember how much the guinea pig has done for us.

Probably the last creatures that anyone thinks of as domesticated animals are mice and rats. Yet they are among the most domesticated in the sense that we have changed them to do specific work. In laboratories around the world, white mice and rats help scientists learn how different foods and medicines work. One *strain* of rats has been developed that has a tendency to get arthritis and another that has heart problems, for example. The arthritic rats help scientists find ways to treat the condition in humans. The rats with heart defects might be put on different diets to see how food affects their health. Rats and mice with the tendency to get cancer help in the discovery of cures. Like other domestic animals, rats and mice didn't volunteer, and we shouldn't forget to be grateful for their help.

11

Elephant Warriors and Workers

Imagine you're a young boy living in India, and your father has just told you that you've been assigned to a five-year-old elephant calf. You're going to learn to be a mahout. You've watched your older brother grow up with his elephant and become a good elephant driver. You've envied the way he rides so easily on his elephant's neck and gives commands with his feet. He can tell the elephant to go right or left with a slight pressure from his foot behind the elephant's ear. A touch on its head tells the elephant to kneel, and a touch on its back says stop. You know how much your father loves the elephant he's worked with since he was a boy. But now it's your turn, and you wonder if you can do it. You can hear the young elephant trumpet and scream as the men push it into a cage for its first lessons. Your elephant doesn't want to go to school! What will happen when you are lowered onto the calf's back? Will this frightened elephant learn to trust you?

In three years your elephant will carry light loads, and five years later, it will begin to drag heavy logs from deep in the rain forest. By then it must know what you mean when you call, "Lift the chain" and "Climb over the log" and "Smash the obstacle." For the first time you think about the first person who tamed an elephant long ago. How brave he must have been!

Elephants were crop robbers in a big way. They still are. Farmers in Africa have found no fence that can hold back a herd of elephants determined to march through a planted field. People didn't come together gradually with elephants as we did with other animals. Our capture of elephants must have been what one person called a "swift enslavement."

The first swift capture may have happened when one country was going to war. What a surprise for an enemy army on foot or on horseback to come up against a line of monsters. About four thousand years ago, elephants were used like heavy tanks. But elephants weren't perfect war machines. They need tons of food. They use a lot of energy, and they tire easily. In the logging forests, elephants work three days and rest for two, and they can't work at all during the hottest months. Soldiers in the middle of a battle can't stop to give animals a rest. In the confusion and noise of galloping horses and the shouts of soldiers in battle, war elephants weren't easy to control. How could the elephants tell friend from foe? Often in their rush to get away, the elephants trampled as many of their own soldiers as they did the enemy's.

The most famous military elephants were those of General Hannibal, who marched through Spain, over the high Alpine mountains, and into Italy to fight the Roman army. Thirty-eight elephants carried the supplies. Elephants are sturdy and sure-footed. Their step is so light and quiet that even a five-ton bull elephant scarcely leaves a track. But that wasn't enough to help them in the mountains. After months of terrible hardships, most of Hannibal's elephants, along with forty thousand of his men, were buried by avalanches that roared into the mountain valleys.

In India, wealthy emperors and princes liked to parade their elephants wearing precious jewels and fine robes. Sometimes an elephant's tusks were covered in gold. People loved to watch fights between trained elephants. It was great sport to cheer them on as they battled until one elephant fell. The mahouts always said good-bye to their families before a fight started in case they were killed, and often they were. Usually the elephants were bruised, but they survived. Paintings of these battles show that the pointed ends of both the elephants' tusks had been capped or blunted. There are no more public elephant fights, but elephants in India still march in their splendid robes and decorations for holiday celebrations.

Are elephants really domestic animals? "No," says Scott Riddle, who owns an elephant sanctuary and breeding farm in Arkansas. "They've been tamed and they work for us, but we haven't changed them genetically."

By that he means that elephants breed in captivity, but

they've never been selected for a special appearance or purpose the way dogs or cows or horses are. They work for us because we capture and keep them. Neither their brains nor their bodies got smaller, for example, and there aren't any man-made varieties or breeds. One reason we haven't used selective breeding of course is the fact that it takes so long for an elephant to grow up. A yearling horse can run a race, but an elephant drinks its mother's milk until it is two years old. Elephants may not meet the exact definition of a domestic animal, but they are much too important to leave off a list of animals that have changed the way humans live.

All elephant families are very much alike. Usually the oldest female leads a group of other cows and their calves. The young males stay together in another group, and the old bull elephants travel alone. When two families gather at a water hole, they have a great time greeting each other by trumpeting and whirling in circles.

A cow elephant is pregnant for two years. When her calf is born, she nurses it for another two years, and the calf stays close to her until it is five. The young elephants are also cared for by older sisters and aunts in a kind of kindergarten group. It's only when an elephant has become a teenager of fourteen that it is strong enough to go to work. Some elephant keepers sell calves so they won't have to feed them for all those years before they are useful. One zoo figured that in one year an elephant ate 1,600 loaves of bread, 100,000 pounds of hay, 12,000 pounds of alfalfa, 2,000 potatoes, and 3,000 apples, carrots, and other vegetables. It drank more than 15,500 gallons of water and took extra vitamins and minerals, too.

It's easy to tell the difference between African and Asian elephants. African elephants are larger. They have fan-shaped ears so big that one weighs one hundred pounds. Their foreheads are low, and their backs curve down in a swaybacked look. Their deeply crinkled trunks have two pointed tips that work as well as two fingers. These tips can pick up a single blade of grass. Both the cow and bull African elephants have ivory tusks — the world's biggest teeth. The largest tusk ever measured was eleven and a half feet long and weighed more than two hundred pounds.

Asian elephant

African elephant

The Asian or Indian elephants have smaller, triangular ears, and their smooth trunks have only one tip. Their backs are curved, and their high foreheads have two bumps. Only the bull elephants have tusks. Asian elephants live in rain forests, on grasslands, and even in the lower snow zones of the Himalaya Mountains.

A hunt for work elephants in India is called a *khedda*. Two thousand men called drivers and fifty of their biggest work elephants may spend six weeks surrounding two elephant herds and guiding them toward an enormous corral built of sturdy logs planted deep in the ground. Even in the corral, the two herds do not mix. Mahouts ride their tame elephants into the corral to separate and mark the wild elephants by size. The young elephants chosen for training are taken to the river to drink and bathe for the first time since their capture, and the others are let go.

Water is very important to elephants. They need to wallow in mud and swim to cool off their sensitive skin. An elephant's skin looks tough, but it needs great care to get rid of insects and parasites that settle in the folds and creases. After a bath, an elephant powders itself with dust and cleans its ears with the tip of its trunk.

The first night, and for several days after captive elephants have been separated from their families, their trumpeting, screams, and roars echo through the forests. From far away the free elephants answer with their loud calls. But no one knows how long they continue to stay in touch through their silent

long-distance calls. Like vibrations from distant thunder, these rumbling calls are infrasonic. *Infra* means below. Their calls are pitched below the level of sound the human ear can hear.

Fewer and fewer elephants are captured these days. African elephants are not far from extinction. Ivory hunters killed most of the elephants in North Africa more than a thousand years ago, although there is one small herd in the country of Mali on the southern edge of the Sahara Desert. By the end of the 1800s, all the elephants in South Africa were gone. Only in central Africa are some of the great herds kept safe in national parks.

It's against the law to kill an elephant, but illegal hunters called poachers are still shooting them to get the valuable ivory tusks. And even though it's against the law in most countries to buy ivory, the hunters find places to sell the beautiful tusks. Nobody needs ivory. It is only made into jewelry, billiard balls, and other things that could just as well be made of other materials.

If every hunter could be stopped this minute, elephants in Africa would still be in danger of extinction. The huge territories they once roamed have become smaller and smaller as people have taken over that space. Some of the paths that generations of elephants cleared and followed through forests have been made into roads that go past farms and through towns. Elephants' feeding habits are simple. They eat as much as they want and move on. There is time enough for plants in one area to grow again before the herd returns. But where elephants are limited to smaller territory in parks, there is no time for trees and grass to grow again, and the elephants may starve.

In India and a few other southern Asian countries, elephants still help clear forests where big bulldozers and tractors can't be used. But more and more, faster mechanical equipment is taking over. About the only work left for elephants in our lives is as entertainers. Even though it's a job they've done for two thousand years, since the great circuses of Rome, elephants deserve better. They worked for us when we needed them. It clearly seems time to let these intelligent animals go back to their natural ways. At his sanctuary, Mr. Riddle's goal is to allow any elephant to "live out its days in an atmosphere of respect that all elephants deserve." That's a good idea for elephants everywhere.

12 🐦

Animals That Lost Their Jobs

As the sun rose over the plains of India, a call echoed through the stables: "The emperor wants to go hunting. Ready the cheetahs!"

When the stable boys had saddled the snorting, prancing horses, the keeper of the cheetahs led several of the big cats from their cages. Each cheetah wore a blindfold, and each leapt easily to a cushion that had been secured behind a rider's saddle. The cushion wasn't for the cheetah's comfort but to protect the horse, because a cheetah can't pull in its claws like other cats.

Imagine training a horse to hold still while a cheetah leaps on its back! And imagine training a cheetah to ride on a horse! Some cheetahs rode to the hunt in fancy carriages or wagons.

Four hundred years ago, an emperor in India kept a stable of a thousand tamed cheetahs for hunting gazelles. Gazelles run fast, but the cheetah is the fastest mammal on earth. From a

standing start, it can reach a speed of forty-five miles an hour in two seconds. Most cars can't do that!

When the emperor or his friends wanted to hunt, a cheetah was blindfolded until a gazelle was sighted. At the emperor's signal, the cheetah's blindfold was whisked off so it could dash after the prey.

In the 1920s, somebody thought it would be great sport to race cheetahs against greyhounds. The cheetahs were much faster than the dogs, of course. They could have won in a fair race, but the cheetahs cheated. They didn't bother the dogs, but they took shortcuts across the track, which put an end to that kind of race.

Once cheetahs lived in Africa and in Asia from the Red Sea to India. Today there are few left. By the year 2000, they may be extinct. Would they have survived longer if we had domesticated them instead of only keeping a few as pets and hunters? Could they have been bred for special jobs, such as messengers? Perhaps, but then they would have changed, and they wouldn't be the sleek and wonderful cats that they are.

The Bushmen of the Kalahari region of Africa live very much like the hunters and gatherers of ancient times. Water is scarce in the Kalahari Desert, so the Bushmen still carry valuable water in empty ostrich shells. An ostrich egg weighs more than two dozen chicken eggs, and it tastes every bit as good when it's cooked. The shell is as hard as a thick china bowl, and it's not easy to crack without a hammer or a saw. It seems amazing that an ostrich chick can break through when it hatches.

But it wasn't the eggs that people wanted most from the ostrich. It was the feathers. Instead of flight feathers on its wings, the ostrich has long waving plumes that people loved to use for decorations. The ancient Egyptians collected the feathers and used the ostrich skin to make fine soft leather. During the Middle Ages, knights wore plumes on their armored helmets. There weren't many knights, so they didn't need many ostriches. But in the 1800s, a new fashion began. Women loved to wear the tall plumes of ostrich feathers on their hats and long, snake-shaped boas of ostrich feathers around their necks. Those styles just about wiped out the ostriches in North Africa. The last ostrich in Saudi Arabia was shot in 1948. If it weren't for ostrich farms, the biggest bird in the world would have been extinct by now.

When ostrich feathers were hard to find, the price for the plumes was so high that some people thought they could get rich raising ostriches. Farms sprung up in Africa, France, and Florida. But during World War I, nobody had time to think about feathers, and most ostrich farmers went out of business. Now ostriches are kept on farms for tourists to see. Some places offer ostrich rides on tame birds, which must be exciting because the bird can run about forty miles an hour and leap five feet straight up in the air. But as a domestic animal, the ostrich had a short run.

Alligator farms were big business for a while, too. Wild alligators came close to extinction when too many of them were killed for their skins, which can be made into expensive suitcases and shoes. Then a law was passed that made it a crime to kill wild alligators. Now all alligator leather comes from animals raised on farms. The captive alligators are still wild animals. They're not really domesticated, but they won't become extinct.

Pheasants raised on game farms are released into woods and meadows for hunters. But like ostriches and alligators, the pheasants aren't really domesticated either. They are hatched and let go, no different from the pheasants that hatched in the wild.

In 1660, King Karl of Sweden decided that moose could be used to deliver the mail. Moose live in far northern swampy forests, where their favorite food is tree bark. It's not easy to capture an animal as big as a moose, especially in a swamp.

But they are easily tamed. When they were trained to wear harnesses and carry a rider in a saddle, the moose were faster than horses and stronger than reindeer over the frozen land. Some moose are still at work, but snowmobiles have taken over their jobs in most places.

In the 1970s, a biologist in Finland raised two bottle-fed moose named Pussi and Magnus. He wanted to hitch them to a sleigh. The moose didn't mind the harnesses, halters, and bridles, but they paid no attention to the sleigh behind them. They walked where they pleased just as if they were in a pasture. With the sleigh bumping along behind them, they leapt over creeks and jumped over fences. But if the biologist walked ahead of them, Pussi and Magnus would follow like well-trained dogs. There was one small problem with that, too. After about twenty minutes trotting behind their master, they'd browse in the bushes for a while or lie down in the road to take a nap.

One day the biologist wanted to take Pussi and Magnus to another town to show them off. He dangled fresh cabbage in front of their noses and lured the moose up a ramp into a truck. When he tied their halters to the front wall, the moose would lie down quietly as long as the truck was moving. The biologist thought it would be safe to leave them in his truck overnight when he stopped at a town. It was. But in the morning when the moose heard his familiar voice, the two moose jumped right through the canvas covering and onto the road. People ran in all directions, but as soon as the biologist called them, Pussi and Magnus trotted to him and nuzzled their huge noses under his arms. The advantages of domesticated moose didn't seem worth all the trouble, and Pussi and Magnus were given to a zoo.

Every now and then someone tries to raise zebras for farm work or riding. If the zebras are born in captivity, they are easy to train. They can live comfortably in zoos and perform in circuses. But because they're not as big or as strong as horses, there has been no real need for them as workers.

Cormorants are cousins of the pelicans, and like pelicans, they are good fishers. They can dive to a depth of ten or twelve feet and stay underwater for forty-five seconds before they bob up with a fish. About 1,500 years ago, Japanese fishermen began to use cormorants to help them catch fish, and soon Chinese fishermen did the same. A fisherman trains his cormorants to perch on the edge of the boat. Each bird wears a soft rope or leather collar, which keeps it from swallowing a

fish. After a bird dives and catches a fish, it is pulled back into the boat by a rope tied around its body. The fisherman takes the fish and rewards the bird with a small piece of fish.

When Charles I was king of England in the mid-1600s, he appointed a master of cormorants to take charge of the fishing.

And King Louis XIII of France kept tame cormorants for the pleasure of watching them at work. The few cormorants still working in Asian countries are often only used to show tourists how fishermen once made use of these big birds.

Ferrets are first cousin to the weasel, mink, and mongoose. Two thousand years ago, the skinny, fast-footed ferret was raised to catch rabbits. The Roman emperor Augustus sent ferrets to a nearby island to try to keep down the rabbit population. Toward the end of the 1800s, ferrets were shipped to New Zealand where they not only controlled the runaway rabbits, but made themselves so much at home that they became pests themselves. In England ferrets are still sent down holes to drive out rabbits for hunters to shoot.

It's easy to tame ferrets, if you begin when they are babies. Tame ones have been put to work as tube cleaners. If a very

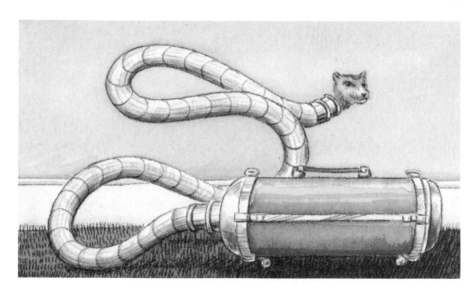

long, narrow tube in a factory has to be cleaned, it's easier to run a ferret through it than to take the tube apart. With a dust cloth fastened to its collar, a ferret can scurry through the narrow tube and come out at the other end for a reward.

But ferrets are best known as pets these days. They make interesting pets if you don't mind the busiest, most curious, energetic animal in the world rummaging through wastebaskets, hiding under cushions, or running up a pant leg. They've been known to explore vacuum cleaner hoses or get tossed into washing machines because they were hiding in the dirty clothes bin. But more difficult to deal with than their high-speed way of life is their odor. Like their skunk cousins, ferrets have musk glands, which is enough to make most people prefer a dog or cat.

Cheetahs, ostriches, alligators, moose, ferrets, cormorants, and zebras didn't make it into the top ranks of important domestic animals because we didn't need them enough. They lost their jobs because what they had to offer was too specialized and not for everyone. Or other animals had already filled those jobs working for people.

13 🐬

Dolphin Divers and
Monkey Butlers

A small capuchin monkey named Hellion leaps from Robert's lap and scampers over to the TV set to turn on the news at noon. Then she opens the refrigerator and takes out a wrapped sandwich, which she carries to the tray on Robert's wheelchair. "Good girl," Robert praises Hellion as she unwraps the sandwich and tosses the paper into the wastebasket. Next she hops onto Robert's lap and gives him a sip of juice from a tube attached to the wheelchair. Then she takes a sip from her own juice bottle. It is her reward.

After lunch, Robert aims a laser pointer at a book he wants, and Hellion gets it for him. While Robert reads, the monkey scoots back to her cage to take a nap. Later in the afternoon, Hellion puts a videotape in the VCR for Robert before she settles in her favorite spot on the windowsill to watch people passing by.

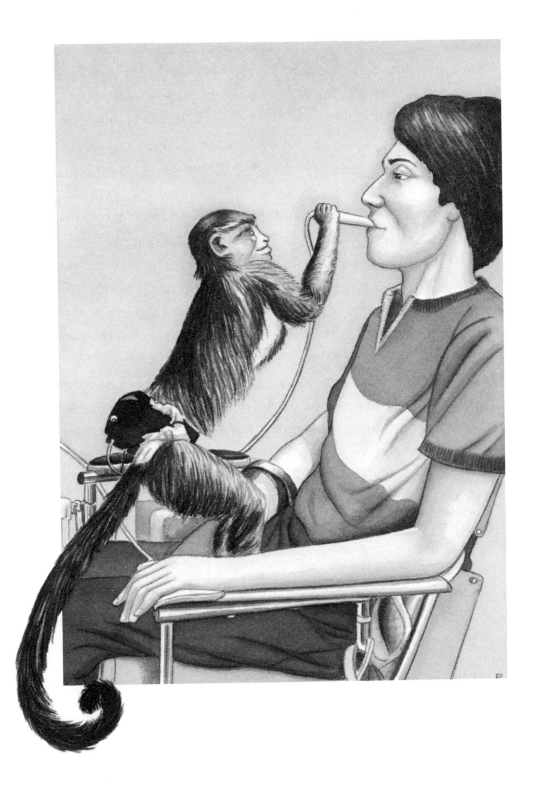

Robert has had to spend his days in a wheelchair since he was in an automobile accident that left his arms and legs paralyzed. He cannot get his own sandwich or turn on a television. He can't even scratch his nose or comb his hair, but Hellion can do these things for him. She's the kind of monkey once used by organ grinders, who stood on street corners, grinding out music from a small organ while a monkey held out a cup for money. But Hellion has a more important job. She works for Helping Hands, an organization that trains monkeys to help disabled people.

Like other capuchin monkeys, Hellion is friendly and quick to learn. The first part of her training began when she was just a baby. In order to get used to living with people, Hellion moved in with a foster family. For the first eight months, Hellion clung to her foster mother or father's arm. Sometimes she nestled in her human mother's apron pocket. For four years, Hellion went wherever her family went — to stores, for rides in the car, and to visit friends.

The hardest part for Hellion was leaving her foster family to go to monkey-helper school in Boston. But it didn't take her long to make new friends. When her teacher showed her a new job, Hellion almost never forgot how to do it. She learned that when her owner-friend aims his small, harmless laser pointer at an object, she is supposed to fetch the object. The laser is mounted on the chin rest that allows Robert to control his electric wheelchair. Robert points the laser by gripping it in his teeth. Sometimes he drops the pointer, but Hellion picks it up and puts it back in his mouth.

She also learned that anything in the house with a round white sticker on it is off limits. This keeps her away from harmful medicine and cleaning supplies, and it keeps her from climbing into cupboards or rummaging through trash cans.

Hellion will spend the rest of her life — maybe thirty years — with her friend Robert. Hundreds more capuchins are being raised for Helping Hands on Discovery Island at Walt Disney World in Florida.

It's easy to see how monkeys can work for us. But how can an animal with no hands and no feet do anything useful?

Dolphins are learning to be our retriever "dogs" of the sea. They certainly are suited to the job. Dolphins can dive down one thousand feet or swim at twenty-five miles an hour. A dolphin can stay underwater longer and battle a shark better than any human diver.

The U.S. Navy has already trained a squadron of dolphins to guard a Trident submarine base. As guards, dolphins are more reliable than the best sonar equipment we have, and they are cheaper. Their pay is only twenty pounds of fish a day and a pat on the head.

Even blindfolded, a dolphin can pick up a dime. At first, dolphins were only asked to pick up tools or other objects from the ocean floor and help in underwater rescues. But in the 1960s, during the Vietnam War, dolphins were trained to ram into objects — such as enemy divers — with barbed darts. One trainer quit because he said it wasn't fair to the dolphins, who thought it was only a game.

In past wars we have used camels, elephants, horses, mules, and donkeys to carry supplies. Homing pigeons and dogs have delivered messages in wartime, and we've even used "watch-dog" geese as guards. But many people agree with the trainer that it's not right to ask the gentle dolphins to become warriors.

Not all domestic animals of the future will be as intelligent and easy to train as monkeys and dolphins. Imagine spiders going to work for people!

The golden orb spider spins silk stronger than anything made by silkworms. It is more sturdy than a thread of steel and tough enough to make into bulletproof vests. But how do you keep a factory full of spiders spinning a steady supply of silk?

Research people worked until they found a microscopic partner for the golden orb spider. It's a bacteria called *E. coli*, a bacteria so common that it's in every person's intestine. Without our *E. coli* partner, humans could not digest food. The researchers were able to combine that bacteria with the spider in a way that solved the problem.

Every living plant and animal has built-in plans that tell each cell what job it will have and how it will do that job. The instructions are contained in *genes*. We have a gene that determines what color eyes we'll have, for example, and another that determines whether we'll have curly hair or straight hair. The golden orb spider has a gene that holds the instructions for making its silk. When scientists found this silk-making gene, they took it out of a spider and joined it to the *E. coli* bacteria. The new bacteria with the gene added can make the silk in a laboratory dish without the spider at all.

Bacteria are neither plants nor animals, but they are alive. They belong to a kingdom of their own called *Monera*. There are thousands of different kinds of bacteria, maybe millions, and all so small that they can only be seen with a microscope. Scientists say that they haven't even come close to discovering all of them. Among the ones we know are bacteria that cause hundreds of different diseases, that spoil food, and that ferment wine. They are the domestic creatures that will help us most in the years ahead because they divide and grow so fast. In half an hour, billions of bacteria can be raised in dishes on a roomful of shelves.

One bacteria has been "built" to gobble up oil spills. Another eats plastic and other kinds of garbage that won't rot or decay. Bacteria are now the factories that make hundreds of medicines, such as insulin to treat a disease called diabetes. Another bacteria can seed a cloud to produce rain.

What other animals could we put to work?

Maybe someone will domesticate bats to kill insects so we won't have to use chemical pesticides. In a night's flight, a bat can eat more than its weight in insects. Every house of the future might have a family of tamed bats that would fly around the yard at night eating insects. At dawn, they'd come back home to roost. Another pair of bats could be the indoor team assigned to destroy cockroaches and other insects we hate to have in our houses.

Gecko lizards are so famous in Hawaii that they are featured characters on everything from T-shirts to beach bags. Real ones are not easy to see because they work the night shift, but the geckos' cheerful chirps tell you they're on duty gobbling up insects. Another lizard called a skink works the day shift. In Florida and other southern states, there's a tiny insect-eating lizard called the anole, although it's commonly called a chameleon. Sometimes people in New York and other big cities buy anoles or geckos to help them get rid of cockroaches. For people who are nervous about bats, perhaps geckos and anoles could be their domesticated insect traps that would hide away behind the refrigerator when they were off duty.

Maybe we can use sharks for coastal cops. Could they be taught to patrol harbors and beaches without harming swimmers? Could we raise sharks on underwater ranches to supply us with shark steaks and tough sharkskin leather?

In September 1991, a huge, hundred-year experiment called Biosphere II began. (Biosphere I is the earth itself.) For the first two years, eight people will live in a glass-covered world. It is a building eighty-five feet high that stretches over three acres of the Sonora Desert near Tucson, Arizona. The members of the Biosphere team will have radios, television, telephones, computers, and fax machines to stay in touch with the outside world. But they will not leave the Biosphere. They will raise their own food and get rid of their garbage. Even their electricity will be generated in their small world. Nothing but information and sunshine will come from outside. One purpose of the experiment is to find out if this kind of building could work on other planets, where people might live for several years. Another purpose is to find out how our own planet works.

Biosphere was designed to be as much like Earth as possible. There is a small rain forest, a small ocean with a coral reef, a saltwater marsh, a savanna, a swamp, a farm, and a desert. Sealed in with the people are a thousand different kinds of plants and animals, including insects, birds, fish, amphibians, reptiles, small mammals, and some domestic animals.

Like the people who lived thousands of years ago, these eight Biosphere team members are keeping pygmy goats, red jungle fowl, and Vietnamese potbellied pigs. Nothing will be wasted.

Biosphere II

The goats and pigs will eat leftovers, and their waste will become fertilizer for the gardens. Meat will come from chickens and pigs and milk from goats. The animals will depend on the people, and the people will depend on the animals.

We can't live alone on this planet. Without domestic animals, our lives would be far different. Maybe we'd still be hunting and gathering for a living. The domestication of animals was a giant step for humans. It was every bit as important as the discovery of fire or the making of tools. For the first time, people began to control nature instead of just taking from it. After a while, the people who farmed had more than they needed. They could sell or trade their extra crops, animals, milk, cheese, wool, or leather goods. For trading they needed pack animals to get their goods to market. They had to keep records of some kind, and that led to the inventions of counting and writing and money. Where traders, sellers, and buyers met at markets, cities grew. And all because we had formed partnerships with animals.

Animals changed as they became domesticated, but so did we. They gave us more than food, clothing, transportation, entertainment, and friendship. They opened the door to civilization.

Do we give them enough in return?

Glossary

Ancestors: the people from whom we are descended; our forefathers. For example, your great-great-grandfather and grandmother are your ancestors. Animals also have ancestors.

Breed: a variety of animal within a species with characteristics that are inherited. A German shepherd, for example, is a breed of the dog species.

Descendants. the people that come from a particular family or ancestor. You descended from, and you are the descendant of, your great-great-grandparents. Dogs are the descendants of wolves.

Domesticate: to bring under the control of humans; to make an animal usable to humans.

Feral: describes an animal that is now living wild but that was once domesticated or that has domesticated ancestors. The mustangs are feral; they are descendants of domestic horses.

Gene: the part of the cell that contains the information for traits that will be inherited.

Gregarious: living in herds or flocks; fond of company; sociable.

Ice Age: a time of intense arctic cold that began about two and a half million years ago when great sheets of ice covered northern Europe and North America. Eight times, the climate warmed and the ice sheets melted back but then froze and returned again. The last ice sheet retreated only ten thousand years ago.

Inherit: to receive a trait from one's ancestors. For example, an animal can inherit size, color of coat, length of tail, or shape of head.

Mutation: a change in a gene that creates a new trait or characteristic, which can then be inherited.

Precocial: the name given to birds whose young are covered with down and can run about as soon as they have hatched.

Runt: the smallest animal of a litter.

Selective breeding: when humans choose, or select, an animal to breed with another animal for the purpose of getting offspring with certain traits.

Species: a group of animals or plants of the same kind with the same name that can interbreed and produce offspring. All dogs are the same species, for example.

Sterile: not fertile; unable to produce offspring.

Stone Age: an age in the history of humans, beginning a million or more years ago, before the use of metals, when humans made axes, spearheads, choppers, and other tools and weapons from stone.

Strain: a line of ancestors; a group of individuals that are related.

Trait: a structure or a behavior that can be passed on to offspring; a characteristic that can be inherited.

Index